ECUADORIAN COOKBOOK

Traditional Recipes from Ecuador

LIAM LUXE

Copyright © 2023 Liam Luxe

All rights reserved.

INTRODUCTION

Welcome to the "Ecuadorian Cookbook." This book is all about the yummy foods from Ecuador, a country in South America. Ecuador has lots of different foods to try, and you're going to learn how to make them! Ecuadorian food is special because it uses fresh ingredients that come from the country's different regions. These ingredients are put together in a way that makes the food taste really good.
You don't have to be a super chef to use this book. Whether you're already a good cook or just starting out, have fun trying these Ecuadorian recipes. It's like going on a yummy adventure in your own kitchen.
From the start to the end of a meal, there are lots of recipes for you to enjoy. Have fun cooking and eating!

CONTENTS

INTRODUCTION iii

APPETIZERS 1
    Ceviche de Camarones (Shrimp Ceviche) 1
    Humitas (Corn Tamales) 2
    Empanadas de Viento (Cheese-Stuffed Empanadas)...............4
    Bolón de Verde (Plantain and Cheese Balls) 5
    Chifles (Fried Plantain Chips) 6
    Papas a la Huancaína (Potatoes in Cheese Sauce)..................8

SOUPS 10
    Locro de Papa (Potato Soup) 10
    Sopa de Quinua (Quinoa Soup)..11
    Caldo de Bolas de Verde (Green Plantain Dumpling Soup) ...13
    Chupe de Pescado (Fish Chowder) 14
    Sopa de Mariscos (Seafood Soup) 16
    Caldo de Gallina (Chicken Soup) 17

MAIN DISHES 19
    Seco de Pollo (Ecuadorian Chicken Stew) 19
    Fanesca (Easter Soup)..20
    Encebollado de Pescado (Fish and Onion Stew) 23
    Arroz con Pollo (Chicken and Rice) 24
    Llapingachos (Potato Pancakes) 26
    Hornado (Roast Pork) 27
    Cuy Asado (Roasted Guinea Pig) 29
    Cazuela de Mariscos (Seafood Casserole)..............................30

SIDE DISHES 33

Tostones (Fried Green Plantains) 33

Yuca al Mojo (Yuca with Garlic Sauce) 34

Arroz con Coco (Coconut Rice) 35

Mote Pillo (Hominy Corn with Scrambled Eggs) 36

Menestra de Lentejas (Lentil Stew) 37

Espinacas a la Crema (Creamed Spinach) 39

VEGETARIAN AND VEGAN 41

Ensalada de Palmito (Hearts of Palm Salad) 41

Choclo con Queso (Corn with Cheese) 42

Acelga Guisada (Stewed Swiss Chard) 43

Espagueti con Salsa de Maní (Peanut Sauce Pasta) 44

Ensalada de Frutas (Fruit Salad) 45

Arroz con Champiñones (Mushroom Rice) 46

SEAFOOD 48

Corviche (Fish and Peanut Patties) 48

Camarones al Ajillo (Garlic Shrimp) 50

Pescado Encocado (Fish in Coconut Sauce) 51

Arroz Marinero (Seafood Rice) 52

Encocado de Camarones (Shrimp in Coconut Sauce) 54

Ceviche Mixto (Mixed Seafood Ceviche) 56

DESSERTS 58

Tres Leches Cake 58

Arroz con Leche (Rice Pudding) 60

Morocho (Corn Pudding) 61

Dulce de Higos (Fig Jam) 62

Cocadas (Coconut Candies) 63

Suspiros (Meringue Cookies) 64

Higos con Queso (Figs with Cheese) 65

BEVERAGES 67

Chicha 67

Colada Morada 68

Canelazo 70

Jugo de Maracuyá (Passion Fruit Juice) 71

Jugo de Tomate de Árbol (Tree Tomato Juice) 71

Café de Loja (Loja Coffee) 72

SAUCES AND CONDIMENTS 75

Ají (Ecuadorian Hot Sauce) 75

Chimichurri 76

Salsa de Maní (Peanut Sauce) 77

Salsa de Cilantro (Cilantro Sauce) 78

BREAD AND SNACKS 80

Pan de Yuca (Cheese Bread) 80

Pan de Pincho (Skewer Bread) 81

Tortillas de Maíz (Corn Tortillas) 82

Arepas (Cornmeal Patties) 83

PRESERVES 86

Mermelada de Guayaba (Guava Jam) 86

Mermelada de Tomate de Árbol (Tree Tomato Jam) 87

HOLIDAY SPECIALTIES 89

Rosca de Pascua (Easter Bread) 89

Colada Morada (Day of the Dead Beverage) 91

Guaguas de Pan (Bread Babies for All Souls' Day) 92

COCKTAILS 95

   Pisco Sour 95

   Caipirinha...96

   Margarita de Maracuyá (Passion Fruit Margarita).............................96

CONVERSION TABLES...98

APPETIZERS

Ceviche de Camarones (Shrimp Ceviche)

Servings: 4-6 **Preparation Time:** 30 minutes (plus chilling time)
Ingredients:
- 1 pound (450g) medium-sized shrimp, peeled and deveined
- 1 red onion, thinly sliced
- 2-3 tomatoes, diced
- 2-3 fresh limes, juiced
- 2-3 fresh lemons, juiced
- 1 orange, juiced
- 1-2 cloves garlic, minced
- 1/2 cup fresh cilantro leaves, chopped
- 1-2 fresh aji peppers (or substitute with jalapeño or serrano peppers), finely chopped (adjust to your spice preference)
- Salt and pepper to taste
- 1-2 tablespoons ketchup (optional, for a touch of sweetness)
- Corn kernels (optional, for garnish)
- Plantain chips or corn nuts (optional, for serving)

Instructions:
1. **Prepare the Shrimp:**
- Bring a pot of water to a boil. Add the shrimp and cook for 2-3 minutes until they turn pink and opaque.
- Drain the shrimp and transfer them to a bowl of ice water to stop the cooking process.

- Once cooled, drain again and pat them dry with paper towels.
2. **Marinate the Shrimp:**
- Cut the cooked shrimp into bite-sized pieces and place them in a large mixing bowl.
- Squeeze the fresh lime, lemon, and orange juice over the shrimp, ensuring they are fully submerged. Let the shrimp "cook" in the citrus juices for about 10-15 minutes. They will turn opaque and firm.
3. **Prepare the Vegetables:**
- While the shrimp marinates, thinly slice the red onion, dice the tomatoes, and chop the fresh cilantro leaves.
- If you're using aji peppers, finely chop them. Remember to remove the seeds for less heat or leave them for extra spice.
4. **Assemble the Ceviche:**
- Drain any excess citrus juice from the shrimp, leaving a little to keep it flavorful.
- Add the minced garlic, sliced red onion, diced tomatoes, and chopped cilantro to the shrimp.
- Season with salt, pepper, and a touch of ketchup if you prefer a slightly sweet taste.
5. **Mix It Up:**
- Gently toss all the ingredients together to ensure they are well combined. Taste and adjust the seasoning as needed, adding more lime juice or salt if desired.
6. **Chill and Serve:**
- Cover the ceviche with plastic wrap and refrigerate for at least 30 minutes to let the flavors meld together. It can be chilled for several hours if desired.
- Just before serving, garnish with corn kernels for a pop of color and crunch.
- Serve your Ceviche de Camarones with plantain chips or corn nuts for a satisfying crunch. Enjoy!

This refreshing and zesty Shrimp Ceviche is a beloved Ecuadorian classic. It's perfect as an appetizer, light meal, or a refreshing snack on a warm day.

Humitas (Corn Tamales)

Servings: 8-10 humitas **Preparation Time:** 1 hour (plus soaking time) **Cooking Time:** 40-45 minutes

Ingredients:
- 2 cups fresh corn kernels (about 4-5 ears of corn)
- 1 cup masa harina (corn flour for tamales)
- 1/2 cup vegetable oil or melted butter
- 1/4 cup milk
- 1/4 cup grated queso fresco or feta cheese
- 2 tablespoons sugar (optional, for a slightly sweet flavor)
- 1 teaspoon baking powder
- 1/2 teaspoon salt (adjust to taste)
- 8-10 corn husks, soaked in warm water for 30 minutes and dried

Instructions:

1. **Prepare the Corn:**
   - If using fresh corn, remove the kernels from the cobs. You can use a knife or a grater to do this. Reserve about 1/2 cup of whole kernels for later.

2. **Blend the Corn Mixture:**
   - In a blender or food processor, combine the majority of the corn kernels (about 1.5 cups), masa harina, vegetable oil or melted butter, milk, grated cheese, sugar (if using), baking powder, and salt.
   - Blend until you have a smooth, thick batter. If it's too thick, you can add a little more milk to reach the right consistency.

3. **Mix in Whole Corn Kernels:**
   - Transfer the blended mixture to a bowl and fold in the reserved whole corn kernels. This adds texture to the humitas.

4. **Assemble the Humitas:**
   - Take a soaked corn husk and place it on a clean surface with the pointed end facing you.
   - Spoon about 1/4 cup of the corn mixture onto the center of the husk.

5. **Fold and Tie:**
   - Fold the sides of the corn husk over the filling to enclose it.
   - Fold up the pointed end and tie the humita with a thin strip of corn husk or kitchen twine to secure it.

6. **Steam the Humitas:**
   - Arrange the humitas upright in a large steamer or a pot with a steaming rack.
   - Steam them over simmering water for about 40-45 minutes, or until they become firm and easily separate from the husks when

touched.
7. **Serve:**
- Let the humitas cool for a few minutes before serving. They can be enjoyed warm or at room temperature.

Humitas are a delightful Ecuadorian treat enjoyed as a snack or side dish.

Empanadas de Viento (Cheese-Stuffed Empanadas)

Servings: 10-12 empanadas **Preparation Time:** 30 minutes **Cooking Time:** 15-20 minutes

Ingredients:

For the Dough:
- 2 cups all-purpose flour
- 1 teaspoon baking powder
- 1/2 teaspoon salt
- 1/4 cup unsalted butter, cold and diced
- 1/4 cup vegetable oil
- 1/2 cup water, approximately (adjust as needed)

For the Filling:
- 1 cup queso fresco or mozzarella cheese, cubed or shredded
- 1/4 cup sugar (for dusting, optional)
- Vegetable oil, for frying

Instructions:

Prepare the Dough:
1. In a mixing bowl, combine the all-purpose flour, baking powder, and salt.
2. Add the cold, diced unsalted butter to the dry ingredients. Use your fingers or a pastry cutter to work the butter into the flour until the mixture resembles coarse crumbs.
3. Gradually add the vegetable oil and mix it in until the dough starts coming together.
4. Slowly add water, a little at a time, while mixing, until the dough forms a smooth ball. You may not need all the water, so add it sparingly.
5. Knead the dough for a few minutes until it becomes elastic and easy to handle. Then, cover it with a clean kitchen towel and let it rest for about 15-20 minutes.

Prepare the Filling:
6. While the dough is resting, cut the queso fresco or mozzarella cheese into small cubes or shred it.

Shape and Fill the Empanadas:
7. Divide the dough into 10-12 equal portions and roll each one into a ball.
8. Take one dough ball and roll it out into a circle about 4-5 inches in diameter. The dough should be thin but not too thin.
9. Place a cube or a small amount of shredded cheese in the center of the dough circle.
10. Fold the dough over the cheese to form a half-moon shape. Press the edges firmly to seal.

Fry the Empanadas:
11. Heat vegetable oil in a deep skillet or frying pan over medium-high heat until it reaches 350°F (175°C).
12. Carefully place the empanadas in the hot oil, a few at a time, and fry until they turn golden brown, about 2-3 minutes per side.
13. Using a slotted spoon, remove the empanadas from the oil and place them on a plate lined with paper towels to drain any excess oil.

Serve and Enjoy:
14. If desired, dust the hot empanadas with sugar for a sweet touch.
15. Empanadas de Viento are best enjoyed warm. Serve them as a snack or dessert, and savor the crispy, cheesy goodness!

These Cheese-Stuffed Empanadas are a delightful Ecuadorian treat, perfect for satisfying your cravings for something savory and cheesy.

Bolón de Verde (Plantain and Cheese Balls)

Servings: 6-8 bolones **Preparation Time:** 30 minutes **Cooking Time:** 15-20 minutes

Ingredients:
- 4 ripe green plantains
- 1 cup queso fresco or mozzarella cheese, grated
- 1/4 cup chicharrones or cooked bacon bits (optional, for added flavor)
- 1/4 cup finely chopped fresh cilantro
- 1/4 cup finely chopped green onions or chives
- Salt and pepper to taste

- Vegetable oil, for frying

Instructions:

Prepare the Plantains:

1. Start by peeling the green plantains. Cut them into chunks for easier blending.
2. In a food processor or blender, pulse the plantain chunks until you have a thick, smooth dough-like consistency. If needed, you can add a tablespoon or two of water to help with blending.

Mix the Ingredients:

3. Transfer the blended plantains to a mixing bowl. Add the grated cheese, chicharrones or bacon bits (if using), chopped cilantro, and chopped green onions or chives.
4. Season the mixture with salt and pepper to taste. Remember that the cheese and chicharrones (if used) already have some saltiness, so go easy on the salt at first and adjust as needed.
5. Use your hands to knead and mix all the ingredients thoroughly. The mixture should be firm and easy to handle.

Shape the Bolones:

6. Take a small handful of the plantain mixture and flatten it in your hand.
7. Place a small cube of queso fresco or mozzarella cheese in the center.
8. Mold the plantain mixture around the cheese, shaping it into a round ball. Make sure the cheese is completely enclosed.

Fry the Bolones:

9. Heat vegetable oil in a deep skillet or frying pan over medium-high heat until it reaches 350°F (175°C).
10. Carefully place the bolones in the hot oil, a few at a time, and fry until they turn golden brown, about 3-4 minutes per side.
11. Using a slotted spoon, remove the bolones from the oil and place them on a plate lined with paper towels to drain any excess oil.

Serve and Enjoy:

12. Bolón de Verde is best enjoyed warm. Serve them as a snack or side dish, and savor the crispy outside and gooey, cheesy inside!

These Plantain and Cheese Balls are a beloved Ecuadorian treat, perfect for satisfying your cravings for a delicious and savory snack.

Chifles (Fried Plantain Chips)

Servings: 4-6 **Preparation Time:** 15 minutes **Cooking Time:** 15

minutes

Ingredients:
- 3-4 green (unripe) plantains
- Vegetable oil, for frying
- Salt, to taste

Instructions:

Prepare the Plantains:
1. Start by peeling the green plantains. Use a knife to carefully slice off the ends of each plantain, then make a shallow cut lengthwise along the skin. Gently remove the skin by wedging your thumb or a spoon between the skin and the flesh.
2. Slice the peeled plantains into very thin rounds. You can use a knife or a mandoline slicer for this. Aim for slices about 1/16 to 1/8 inch thick.

Fry the Chifles:
3. Heat vegetable oil in a deep skillet or frying pan over medium-high heat until it reaches 350°F (175°C).
4. Carefully add a batch of the sliced plantains to the hot oil. Be cautious to avoid overcrowding the pan, as the chips need space to cook evenly.
5. Fry the plantain slices for about 3-4 minutes, or until they turn golden brown and crispy. Stir occasionally to ensure even frying.
6. Using a slotted spoon or tongs, remove the fried plantain chips from the oil and place them on a plate lined with paper towels to drain any excess oil.
7. Sprinkle the hot chifles with salt to taste while they are still oily. You can be generous with the salt or adjust according to your preference.
8. Repeat the frying process with the remaining plantain slices until they are all crispy and golden.

Serve and Enjoy:
9. Chifles are best enjoyed fresh and warm. Serve them as a snack or side dish with your favorite dipping sauces or alongside other Ecuadorian dishes.

These crispy Fried Plantain Chips, known as Chifles, are a popular snack in Ecuador and across many Latin American countries. Their simplicity and addictively salty, crunchy texture make them a delightful treat.

Papas a la Huancaína (Potatoes in Cheese Sauce)

Servings: 4-6 **Preparation Time:** 30 minutes **Cooking Time:** 15 minutes

Ingredients:

For the Huancaina Sauce:
- 1 cup queso fresco or feta cheese, crumbled
- 4-5 aji amarillo peppers (or substitute with yellow chili peppers or aji amarillo paste, adjust to your spice preference)
- 2 cloves garlic, minced
- 1 cup evaporated milk
- 1/2 cup vegetable oil
- Salt and pepper to taste
- 1-2 sleeves of soda crackers or saltine crackers (about 20-25 crackers)
- 4-5 black olives, pitted and halved (for garnish, optional)
- 2 hard-boiled eggs, sliced (for garnish, optional)
- Lettuce leaves (for serving, optional)

For the Potatoes:
- 4-6 large yellow or white potatoes, peeled and boiled until fork-tender
- Lettuce leaves (for serving, optional)

Instructions:

Prepare the Huancaina Sauce:
1. In a blender or food processor, combine the crumbled queso fresco or feta cheese, aji amarillo peppers, minced garlic, evaporated milk, and vegetable oil.
2. Blend until you have a smooth and creamy sauce. If the sauce is too thick, you can add a little more evaporated milk to reach the desired consistency.
3. Crush the soda crackers or saltine crackers into fine crumbs and add them to the blender. This will help thicken the sauce.
4. Blend again until the crackers are fully incorporated into the sauce.
5. Taste the sauce and season with salt and pepper as needed. Adjust the spiciness by adding more aji amarillo peppers if desired.

Prepare the Potatoes:

6. Peel and boil the potatoes in salted water until they are fork-tender. Drain and let them cool slightly.
7. Cut the boiled potatoes into thick slices and arrange them on a serving platter lined with lettuce leaves (if using).

Assemble and Serve:
8. Pour the Huancaina sauce generously over the potato slices.
9. Garnish with halved black olives and slices of hard-boiled egg, if desired.
10. Serve the Papas a la Huancaína as an appetizer or a light meal. You can also accompany it with more lettuce leaves on the side.
11. Enjoy this creamy and mildly spicy dish that's a true Ecuadorian classic!

SOUPS

Locro de Papa (Potato Soup)

Servings: 4-6 **Preparation Time:** 30 minutes **Cooking Time:** 30-40 minutes

Ingredients:
- 4-5 large yellow potatoes, peeled and cut into chunks
- 1 cup queso fresco or mozzarella cheese, cubed or shredded
- 1 cup milk
- 1/2 cup heavy cream (or substitute with more milk)
- 1 onion, finely chopped
- 2 cloves garlic, minced
- 2 tablespoons vegetable oil
- 2 tablespoons butter
- 1 teaspoon ground cumin
- 1/2 teaspoon achiote or annatto powder (for color, optional)
- Salt and pepper to taste
- Fresh cilantro leaves, chopped (for garnish, optional)
- Avocado slices (for garnish, optional)
- Toasted corn kernels (cancha, optional, for garnish)

Instructions:

Cook the Potatoes:

1. In a large pot, heat the vegetable oil over medium heat. Add the chopped onion and minced garlic. Sauté until they become soft and translucent.

2. Stir in the ground cumin and achiote powder (if using) to infuse the oil with flavor.
3. Add the peeled and chunked yellow potatoes to the pot. Stir them to coat with the onion and spice mixture.
4. Pour in enough water to cover the potatoes by about an inch. Season with salt and pepper to taste.
5. Bring the mixture to a boil, then reduce the heat to low and simmer for about 20-25 minutes, or until the potatoes are fork-tender and easily mashed.

Mash the Potatoes:
6. Using a potato masher or the back of a spoon, mash some of the potatoes in the pot. This will help thicken the soup while leaving some potato chunks for texture.

Prepare the Creamy Base:
7. Pour in the milk and heavy cream (or additional milk) into the pot. Stir well to combine.
8. Add the cubed or shredded queso fresco or mozzarella cheese and butter. Continue to stir until the cheese is melted and the soup becomes creamy. If needed, you can add more milk to reach your desired consistency.
9. Taste the soup and adjust the seasoning with more salt and pepper if necessary.

Serve and Garnish:
10. Ladle the Locro de Papa into bowls.
11. Garnish each bowl with chopped fresh cilantro leaves, avocado slices, and toasted corn kernels (cancha) if desired.
12. Serve this comforting Ecuadorian Potato Soup hot and enjoy the creamy, cheesy goodness!

Sopa de Quinua (Quinoa Soup)

Servings: 4-6 **Preparation Time:** 15 minutes **Cooking Time:** 30-35 minutes

Ingredients:
- 1 cup quinoa, rinsed and drained
- 1 cup cooked chicken, shredded (optional)
- 1 small onion, finely chopped
- 2 cloves garlic, minced
- 2 tablespoons vegetable oil
- 1 large carrot, diced

- 1 large potato, diced
- 1/2 cup green peas (fresh or frozen)
- 1/2 cup corn kernels (fresh or frozen)
- 6 cups chicken or vegetable broth
- 1/2 teaspoon ground cumin
- 1/2 teaspoon dried oregano
- Salt and pepper to taste
- Fresh cilantro leaves, chopped (for garnish, optional)
- Lime or lemon wedges (for serving, optional)

Instructions:

Sauté the Vegetables:
1. In a large pot, heat the vegetable oil over medium heat. Add the chopped onion and minced garlic. Sauté until they become soft and translucent.
2. Stir in the ground cumin and dried oregano to infuse the oil with flavor.

Add the Vegetables and Quinoa:
3. Add the diced carrot, potato, green peas, and corn kernels to the pot. Stir them to combine with the sautéed onions and spices.
4. Pour in the rinsed and drained quinoa. Stir it into the vegetable mixture.

Simmer the Soup:
5. Pour in the chicken or vegetable broth, ensuring that the vegetables and quinoa are fully submerged.
6. Bring the soup to a boil, then reduce the heat to low and simmer for about 20-25 minutes, or until the quinoa is cooked and the vegetables are tender.

Add Chicken (Optional) and Season:
7. If using cooked chicken, add it to the soup and stir to heat through.
8. Season the soup with salt and pepper to taste. Adjust the seasoning according to your preference.

Serve and Garnish:
9. Ladle the Sopa de Quinua into bowls.
10. Garnish each bowl with chopped fresh cilantro leaves and a wedge of lime or lemon if desired. The citrus adds a refreshing twist to the soup.
11. Serve this nutritious and hearty Quinoa Soup hot and enjoy the comforting flavors of Ecuador!

Caldo de Bolas de Verde (Green Plantain Dumpling Soup)

Servings: 4-6 **Preparation Time:** 45 minutes **Cooking Time:** 45 minutes

Ingredients:

For the Dumplings (Bolas de Verde):
- 2-3 green (unripe) plantains, peeled and roughly chopped
- 1 cup queso fresco or mozzarella cheese, grated
- 1/4 cup finely chopped fresh cilantro
- 1/4 cup finely chopped green onions or chives
- Salt and pepper to taste
- 1-2 teaspoons achiote or annatto powder (for color, optional)
- 1 egg (for binding, optional)
- Cornstarch (for dusting)

For the Soup:
- 8 cups chicken or vegetable broth
- 2 cups mixed vegetables (carrots, peas, corn, green beans, etc.)
- 1 onion, finely chopped
- 2 cloves garlic, minced
- 2 tablespoons vegetable oil
- 1 teaspoon ground cumin
- 1/2 teaspoon dried oregano
- Salt and pepper to taste
- Fresh cilantro leaves, chopped (for garnish, optional)
- Lime or lemon wedges (for serving, optional)

Instructions:

Prepare the Dumplings (Bolas de Verde):
1. In a pot of boiling water, cook the chopped green plantains until they are tender, about 10-15 minutes.
2. Drain the cooked plantains and let them cool slightly.
3. Mash the cooked plantains using a potato masher or a fork. They should be smooth and free of lumps.
4. Add the grated queso fresco or mozzarella cheese, finely chopped cilantro, green onions or chives, and optional achiote or annatto powder for color.
5. Season the mixture with salt and pepper to taste.
6. If the mixture is not binding well, you can add an egg to help

hold it together.
7. Sprinkle some cornstarch on a clean surface to prevent sticking. Take a small portion of the mixture and shape it into a ball or dumpling. Repeat until all the mixture is used. You should have around 12-15 dumplings.

Prepare the Soup:
8. In a large pot, heat the vegetable oil over medium heat. Add the finely chopped onion and minced garlic. Sauté until they become soft and translucent.
9. Stir in the ground cumin and dried oregano to infuse the oil with flavor.
10. Pour in the chicken or vegetable broth and bring it to a boil.
11. Add the mixed vegetables to the broth and simmer for about 10 minutes, or until they are tender.
12. Carefully add the prepared dumplings (Bolas de Verde) to the simmering soup. Cook for another 15-20 minutes, or until the dumplings are cooked through. They will float to the surface when done.
13. Season the soup with salt and pepper to taste. Adjust the seasoning according to your preference.

Serve and Garnish:
14. Ladle the Caldo de Bolas de Verde into bowls.
15. Garnish each bowl with chopped fresh cilantro leaves and a wedge of lime or lemon if desired. The citrus adds a refreshing twist to the soup.
16. Serve this Ecuadorian Green Plantain Dumpling Soup hot and enjoy the comforting and flavorful combination of dumplings and broth!

Chupe de Pescado (Fish Chowder)

Servings: 4-6 **Preparation Time:** 20 minutes **Cooking Time:** 30-35 minutes

Ingredients:
- 1 pound white fish fillets (such as tilapia or cod), cut into bite-sized pieces
- 1 onion, finely chopped
- 2 cloves garlic, minced
- 2 tablespoons vegetable oil
- 1 red bell pepper, diced

- 1 yellow bell pepper, diced
- 1 cup frozen or fresh corn kernels
- 1 cup green peas (fresh or frozen)
- 1 cup diced carrots
- 1 cup diced potatoes
- 4 cups fish or vegetable broth
- 1 cup evaporated milk
- 1/2 cup fresh white cheese (queso fresco), crumbled
- 2 tablespoons aji amarillo paste or yellow chili sauce (adjust to your spice preference)
- 1/2 teaspoon ground cumin
- Salt and pepper to taste
- Fresh cilantro leaves, chopped (for garnish, optional)
- Lime or lemon wedges (for serving, optional)

Instructions:

Sauté the Vegetables:

1. In a large pot, heat the vegetable oil over medium heat. Add the finely chopped onion and minced garlic. Sauté until they become soft and translucent.
2. Stir in the diced red and yellow bell peppers, corn kernels, green peas, diced carrots, and diced potatoes. Cook for a few minutes to soften the vegetables.

Add the Broth and Seasonings:

3. Pour in the fish or vegetable broth, ensuring that the vegetables are fully submerged.
4. Add the aji amarillo paste or yellow chili sauce for a touch of heat and ground cumin for flavor.
5. Season the soup with salt and pepper to taste. Adjust the seasoning according to your preference.

Cook the Fish:

6. Gently add the bite-sized pieces of fish to the simmering soup. Cook for about 5-7 minutes, or until the fish is opaque and flakes easily.

Finish the Chowder:

7. Pour in the evaporated milk to create a creamy base for the chowder. Stir well to combine.
8. Add the crumbled fresh white cheese (queso fresco) to the chowder. Stir until the cheese is melted and the chowder becomes creamy.

Serve and Garnish:
9. Ladle the Chupe de Pescado into bowls.
10. Garnish each bowl with chopped fresh cilantro leaves and a wedge of lime or lemon if desired. The citrus adds a refreshing twist to the chowder.
11. Serve this hearty and flavorful Fish Chowder hot and enjoy the delightful combination of fish, vegetables, and creamy broth!

Sopa de Mariscos (Seafood Soup)

Servings: 4-6 **Preparation Time:** 20 minutes **Cooking Time:** 30-35 minutes

Ingredients:
- 1 pound mixed seafood (shrimp, squid, mussels, and white fish fillets), cleaned and cut into bite-sized pieces
- 1 onion, finely chopped
- 2 cloves garlic, minced
- 2 tablespoons vegetable oil
- 1 red bell pepper, diced
- 1 yellow bell pepper, diced
- 1 cup diced tomatoes (fresh or canned)
- 1/2 cup white wine (optional)
- 4 cups fish or seafood broth
- 1 cup coconut milk
- 1 tablespoon tomato paste
- 1 teaspoon ground cumin
- 1/2 teaspoon paprika
- 1/2 teaspoon dried oregano
- Salt and pepper to taste
- Fresh cilantro leaves, chopped (for garnish, optional)
- Lime or lemon wedges (for serving, optional)

Instructions:
Sauté the Vegetables:
1. In a large pot, heat the vegetable oil over medium heat. Add the finely chopped onion and minced garlic. Sauté until they become soft and translucent.
2. Stir in the diced red and yellow bell peppers and cook for a few minutes to soften them.

Add the Tomatoes and Wine (Optional):
3. Add the diced tomatoes to the pot. If using white wine, pour it in

as well. Cook for a couple of minutes to allow the alcohol to evaporate.
Add the Broth and Seasonings:
4. Pour in the fish or seafood broth, ensuring that the vegetables are fully submerged.
5. Add the tomato paste, ground cumin, paprika, dried oregano, salt, and pepper to taste. Stir well to combine.
Simmer the Soup:
6. Bring the soup to a simmer and cook for about 15-20 minutes, allowing the flavors to meld together.
Add the Seafood:
7. Gently add the bite-sized pieces of mixed seafood to the simmering soup. Cook for about 5-7 minutes, or until the seafood is cooked through. Be careful not to overcook, as seafood can become tough if cooked too long.
Finish the Soup:
8. Pour in the coconut milk to create a creamy and rich base for the soup. Stir until well incorporated.
Serve and Garnish:
9. Ladle the Sopa de Mariscos into bowls.
10. Garnish each bowl with chopped fresh cilantro leaves and a wedge of lime or lemon if desired. The citrus adds a refreshing twist to the soup.
11. Serve this exquisite and flavorful Seafood Soup hot and savor the delightful combination of tender seafood, aromatic spices, and creamy coconut milk!

Caldo de Gallina (Chicken Soup)

Servings: 4-6 **Preparation Time:** 15 minutes **Cooking Time:** 1 hour 30 minutes

Ingredients:
- 1 whole chicken (about 3-4 pounds), cut into pieces
- 1 onion, finely chopped
- 2 cloves garlic, minced
- 2 tablespoons vegetable oil
- 2 carrots, peeled and sliced
- 2 potatoes, peeled and diced
- 1 cup green peas (fresh or frozen)
- 1 cup corn kernels (fresh or frozen)

- 1 cup diced yuca or cassava (optional)
- 1/2 cup rice (optional)
- 8 cups chicken broth
- 1/2 teaspoon ground cumin
- 1/2 teaspoon dried oregano
- Salt and pepper to taste
- Fresh cilantro leaves, chopped (for garnish, optional)
- Lime or lemon wedges (for serving, optional)

Instructions:

Sauté the Vegetables:

1. In a large pot, heat the vegetable oil over medium heat. Add the finely chopped onion and minced garlic. Sauté until they become soft and translucent.
2. Stir in the sliced carrots, diced potatoes, green peas, corn kernels, and diced yuca or cassava (if using). Cook for a few minutes to soften the vegetables.

Add the Chicken and Seasonings:

3. Add the chicken pieces to the pot. Cook for a few minutes to brown the chicken slightly.
4. Season the mixture with ground cumin, dried oregano, salt, and pepper to taste. Stir well to coat the ingredients with the spices.

Simmer the Soup:

5. Pour in the chicken broth, ensuring that the chicken and vegetables are fully submerged.
6. If using rice, add it to the pot. Stir to combine.
7. Bring the soup to a boil, then reduce the heat to low, cover, and simmer for about 1 hour, or until the chicken is tender and the flavors have melded together. Skim off any impurities that rise to the surface.

Serve and Garnish:

8. Ladle the Caldo de Gallina into bowls.
9. Garnish each bowl with chopped fresh cilantro leaves and a wedge of lime or lemon if desired. The citrus adds a refreshing twist to the soup.
10. Serve this comforting and nourishing Chicken Soup hot and enjoy the delicious combination of tender chicken, hearty vegetables, and aromatic spices!

MAIN DISHES

Seco de Pollo (Ecuadorian Chicken Stew)

Servings: 4-6 **Preparation Time:** 15 minutes **Cooking Time:** 45 minutes

Ingredients:
For the Chicken Marinade:
- 2-3 pounds chicken pieces (legs and thighs are commonly used)
- 2 cloves garlic, minced
- 1 teaspoon ground cumin
- 1/2 teaspoon paprika
- 1/2 teaspoon ground achiote (annatto) or achiote paste (for color, optional)
- Salt and pepper to taste
- Juice of 1 lime or lemon

For the Stew:
- 2 tablespoons vegetable oil
- 1 onion, finely chopped
- 2 cloves garlic, minced
- 2 tomatoes, finely chopped
- 1 bell pepper (red or green), diced
- 2 cups cooked white rice (for serving)
- 2 cups cooked lentils (for serving)
- 1 cup water
- 1/2 cup beer or chicken broth

- 1/2 cup fresh cilantro leaves, chopped
- Salt and pepper to taste

Instructions:
Marinate the Chicken:
1. In a bowl, combine the minced garlic, ground cumin, paprika, ground achiote (if using), salt, pepper, and the juice of one lime or lemon.
2. Rub the chicken pieces with this marinade, ensuring they are well coated. Allow the chicken to marinate for at least 30 minutes, or refrigerate it for a few hours to enhance the flavor.

Cook the Chicken:
3. In a large pot or Dutch oven, heat the vegetable oil over medium-high heat. Add the marinated chicken pieces and sear them until they are browned on all sides. This should take about 5-7 minutes. Remove the chicken from the pot and set it aside.

Prepare the Stew:
4. In the same pot, add the finely chopped onion and minced garlic. Sauté until they become soft and translucent.
5. Stir in the finely chopped tomatoes and diced bell pepper. Cook for a few minutes until the vegetables begin to soften.
6. Return the seared chicken to the pot.
7. Pour in the water, beer or chicken broth. This will help create a flavorful and aromatic sauce.
8. Cover the pot, reduce the heat to low, and simmer for about 30-35 minutes, or until the chicken is tender and cooked through. Stir occasionally to prevent sticking.
9. Season the stew with salt and pepper to taste. Adjust the seasoning according to your preference.

Serve the Seco de Pollo:
10. To serve, place a scoop of cooked white rice and cooked lentils on each plate.
11. Spoon the Seco de Pollo over the rice and lentils.
12. Garnish with freshly chopped cilantro leaves.

Fanesca (Easter Soup)

Servings: 8-10 **Preparation Time:** 30 minutes **Cooking Time:** 1 hour 30 minutes

Ingredients:
For the Soup Base:

- 1 cup dried fava beans (habas), soaked overnight
- 1 cup dried white corn (mote), soaked overnight
- 2 tablespoons vegetable oil
- 1 onion, finely chopped
- 3 cloves garlic, minced
- 1 teaspoon ground cumin
- 1/2 teaspoon ground achiote (annatto) or achiote paste (for color, optional)
- 1/2 teaspoon dried oregano
- 8 cups milk (whole or 2%)
- 2 cups water
- Salt and pepper to taste

For the Filling:
- 1/2 cup dried salted cod (bacalao), soaked and desalted, shredded
- 1/2 cup cooked rice
- 1/2 cup cooked lentils
- 1/2 cup cooked chickpeas
- 1/2 cup cooked white beans
- 1/2 cup cooked green peas
- 1/2 cup diced pumpkin or squash
- 1/2 cup diced sweet potato
- 1/2 cup diced zucchini
- 1/2 cup diced carrot
- 1/2 cup diced green plantain
- 1/2 cup diced yellow plantain
- 1/2 cup diced corn on the cob
- 1/2 cup diced queso fresco or mozzarella cheese
- 2 tablespoons finely chopped fresh cilantro
- 2 tablespoons finely chopped fresh parsley
- 1/2 teaspoon ground cumin
- Salt and pepper to taste

For Garnish:
- Hard-boiled eggs, sliced
- Fresh cilantro leaves, chopped
- Fresh parsley leaves, chopped
- Queso fresco or mozzarella cheese, crumbled
- Slices of white cheese
- Aji or hot sauce (optional)
- Toasted corn kernels (cancha, optional)

Instructions:
Prepare the Soup Base:
1. Drain and rinse the soaked fava beans and white corn.
2. In a large pot, heat the vegetable oil over medium heat. Add the finely chopped onion and minced garlic. Sauté until they become soft and translucent.
3. Stir in the ground cumin, dried oregano, and ground achiote (if using) to infuse the oil with flavor.
4. Add the drained fava beans and white corn to the pot. Stir to coat them with the onion and spice mixture.
5. Pour in the milk and water. Bring the mixture to a boil, then reduce the heat to low, cover, and simmer for about 45 minutes to 1 hour, or until the beans and corn are tender.
6. Using an immersion blender or a regular blender (in batches), puree the soup until smooth. Return it to the pot.

Prepare the Filling:
7. In a separate pot, boil the diced pumpkin or squash, sweet potato, zucchini, carrot, green and yellow plantains, and corn on the cob until they are tender. Drain them and set aside.
8. In a large mixing bowl, combine the shredded salted cod (bacalao), cooked rice, cooked lentils, cooked chickpeas, cooked white beans, cooked green peas, and the boiled and diced vegetables.
9. Add the diced queso fresco or mozzarella cheese, finely chopped cilantro, finely chopped parsley, ground cumin, salt, and pepper. Mix everything together thoroughly.

Combine and Serve:
10. Add the prepared filling to the pureed soup in the pot. Stir well to combine.
11. Simmer the soup for an additional 15-20 minutes, allowing the flavors to meld together. Stir occasionally.

Serve Fanesca:
12. Ladle the Fanesca into bowls.
13. Garnish each bowl with slices of hard-boiled eggs, chopped fresh cilantro, chopped fresh parsley, crumbled queso fresco or mozzarella cheese, slices of white cheese, and aji or hot sauce if desired.
14. Optionally, sprinkle toasted corn kernels (cancha) on top for extra crunch and flavor.

Encebollado de Pescado (Fish and Onion Stew)

Servings: 4-6 **Preparation Time:** 20 minutes **Cooking Time:** 30 minutes

Ingredients:

For the Fish Marinade:
- 1 pound fresh tuna or other firm white fish fillets, cut into chunks
- Juice of 2-3 limes or lemons
- Salt and pepper to taste
- 1 teaspoon ground cumin
- 1/2 teaspoon ground achiote (annatto) or achiote paste (for color, optional)

For the Stew:
- 2 tablespoons vegetable oil
- 1 red onion, thinly sliced
- 1 green bell pepper, thinly sliced
- 1 red bell pepper, thinly sliced
- 2 cloves garlic, minced
- 2 tomatoes, finely chopped
- 4 cups fish or seafood broth
- 2 cups water
- 2 tablespoons tomato paste
- 2 tablespoons ketchup
- 1 tablespoon ground cumin
- 1/2 teaspoon dried oregano
- Salt and pepper to taste
- 1/2 cup fresh cilantro leaves, chopped (for garnish)
- 2-3 tablespoons thinly sliced red onion (for garnish)
- 2-3 tablespoons chopped fresh cilantro (for garnish)
- Lime or lemon wedges (for serving)

Instructions:

Marinate the Fish:
1. Place the fish chunks in a bowl and pour the lime or lemon juice over them. Ensure the fish is fully covered. Let it marinate for about 10-15 minutes.
2. Season the fish with salt, pepper, ground cumin, and ground achiote (if using). Toss to coat the fish evenly. Allow it to marinate for an additional 15 minutes while you prepare the stew.

Prepare the Stew:
3. In a large pot, heat the vegetable oil over medium heat. Add the thinly sliced red onion, green bell pepper, and red bell pepper. Sauté until they become soft and translucent.
4. Stir in the minced garlic and cook for an additional minute until fragrant.
5. Add the finely chopped tomatoes and cook for a few minutes until they start to soften.
6. Pour in the fish or seafood broth, water, tomato paste, ketchup, ground cumin, dried oregano, salt, and pepper. Stir well to combine.
7. Bring the stew to a simmer and cook for about 20-25 minutes to allow the flavors to meld together.

Cook the Fish:
8. Gently add the marinated fish to the simmering stew. Cook for about 5-7 minutes, or until the fish is opaque and flakes easily. Be careful not to overcook the fish.

Serve Encebollado de Pescado:
9. Ladle the Encebollado de Pescado into bowls.
10. Garnish each bowl with chopped fresh cilantro leaves, thinly sliced red onion, and chopped fresh cilantro.
11. Serve hot with lime or lemon wedges on the side. Squeeze some citrus juice over the stew before enjoying.

Arroz con Pollo (Chicken and Rice)

Servings: 4-6 **Preparation Time:** 20 minutes **Cooking Time:** 45 minutes

Ingredients:
- 2 cups long-grain white rice
- 4-6 chicken pieces (legs and thighs are commonly used)
- 2 tablespoons vegetable oil
- 1 onion, finely chopped
- 2 cloves garlic, minced
- 1 bell pepper (red or green), diced
- 1 tomato, finely chopped
- 1/2 cup green peas (fresh or frozen)
- 1/2 cup diced carrots
- 1/2 cup diced green beans
- 1/2 cup corn kernels (fresh or frozen)

- 1/2 teaspoon ground cumin
- 1/2 teaspoon paprika
- 1/2 teaspoon saffron threads or saffron powder (for color, optional)
- 4 cups chicken broth
- Salt and pepper to taste
- Fresh cilantro leaves, chopped (for garnish, optional)
- Lime or lemon wedges (for serving, optional)

Instructions:

Rinse and Soak the Rice:
1. Place the rice in a fine-mesh strainer and rinse it under cold running water until the water runs clear. Drain the rice and set it aside.
2. If you're using saffron threads for color, soak them in a few tablespoons of warm water for about 10 minutes.

Brown the Chicken:
3. In a large pot or Dutch oven, heat the vegetable oil over medium-high heat. Add the chicken pieces and brown them on all sides. Remove the chicken from the pot and set it aside.

Sauté the Vegetables:
4. In the same pot, add the finely chopped onion and minced garlic. Sauté until they become soft and translucent.
5. Stir in the diced bell pepper and chopped tomato. Cook for a few minutes until the vegetables begin to soften.

Add the Rice and Spices:
6. Add the rinsed and drained rice to the pot. Stir it into the vegetables and cook for a couple of minutes.
7. Season the mixture with ground cumin, paprika, saffron (if using), salt, and pepper. Stir well to coat the rice and vegetables with the spices.

Combine and Cook:
8. Carefully return the browned chicken pieces to the pot, nestling them into the rice and vegetables.
9. Add the green peas, diced carrots, diced green beans, and corn kernels to the pot.
10. Pour in the chicken broth, ensuring that the rice and chicken are fully submerged.

Simmer and Serve:
11. Bring the mixture to a boil, then reduce the heat to low. Cover

the pot and simmer for about 20-25 minutes, or until the rice is tender and the chicken is cooked through. Check the rice occasionally and add more broth if needed.

Garnish and Enjoy:
12. Once the rice is tender and the chicken is cooked, remove the pot from the heat.
13. Let the Arroz con Pollo rest, covered, for about 10 minutes to allow the flavors to meld.
14. Garnish with chopped fresh cilantro leaves and serve hot with lime or lemon wedges on the side.

Llapingachos (Potato Pancakes)

Servings: 4-6 (makes about 12 pancakes) **Preparation Time:** 30 minutes **Cooking Time:** 20 minutes

Ingredients:
- 4 large russet potatoes, peeled and cut into chunks
- 1/2 cup grated queso fresco or mozzarella cheese
- 1/4 cup finely chopped white onion
- 1/4 cup finely chopped fresh cilantro
- 1/4 cup milk (whole or 2%)
- 2 tablespoons butter
- 1 teaspoon achiote or annatto powder (for color, optional)
- Salt and pepper to taste
- Vegetable oil (for frying)
- 1/2 cup aji criollo (Ecuadorian hot sauce) or aji amarillo sauce (optional, for serving)

Instructions:

Boil and Mash the Potatoes:
1. Place the peeled and chopped potatoes in a large pot of salted boiling water. Cook until they are fork-tender, about 15-20 minutes.
2. Drain the potatoes and return them to the pot. Mash them until they are smooth and free of lumps.

Prepare the Potato Mixture:
3. In a large mixing bowl, combine the mashed potatoes, grated queso fresco or mozzarella cheese, finely chopped white onion, finely chopped fresh cilantro, milk, butter, achiote or annatto powder (if using), salt, and pepper. Mix well until all the ingredients are thoroughly combined. You should have a smooth

potato mixture.

Form the Pancakes:

4. Divide the potato mixture into equal portions and shape them into round, flat pancakes. Traditionally, they are about 3-4 inches in diameter and 1/2 to 1 inch thick.

Pan-Fry the Llapingachos:

5. In a large skillet or frying pan, heat enough vegetable oil over medium-high heat to submerge the pancakes.
6. Carefully place the llapingachos in the hot oil and fry until they are golden brown and crispy on both sides, about 3-4 minutes per side. You may need to do this in batches, depending on the size of your pan.
7. Once cooked, remove the llapingachos from the oil and place them on a plate lined with paper towels to drain any excess oil.

Serve the Llapingachos:

8. Serve the llapingachos hot, garnished with additional queso fresco, fresh cilantro leaves, and aji criollo or aji amarillo sauce (if desired).
9. Enjoy these delicious Ecuadorian Potato Pancakes as a side dish or appetizer, or make them a part of a complete meal by serving them with a protein and a salad.

Hornado (Roast Pork)

Servings: 6-8 **Preparation Time:** 20 minutes (plus marinating time) **Cooking Time:** 4-5 hours

Ingredients:

For the Marinade:
- 1 whole pork leg or shoulder (about 6-8 pounds)
- 6 cloves garlic, minced
- 2 teaspoons ground cumin
- 2 teaspoons dried oregano
- 1 teaspoon ground achiote (annatto) or achiote paste (for color, optional)
- 1/2 cup orange juice
- 1/4 cup lime juice
- Salt and pepper to taste

For the Adobo Sauce:
- 2 red onions, finely chopped
- 2 tablespoons vegetable oil

- 1/4 cup achiote oil (prepared by heating achiote seeds in vegetable oil)
- 2 teaspoons ground cumin
- 2 teaspoons dried oregano
- Salt and pepper to taste

Instructions:

Prepare the Marinade:

1. In a bowl, combine the minced garlic, ground cumin, dried oregano, ground achiote (if using), orange juice, lime juice, salt, and pepper. Mix well to create the marinade.
2. Place the pork leg or shoulder in a large roasting pan or a deep dish. Using a sharp knife, make deep cuts (about 1 inch apart) all over the pork. This will allow the marinade to penetrate and flavor the meat.
3. Pour the marinade over the pork, making sure to rub it into the cuts and all around the meat. Cover the pork with plastic wrap and refrigerate it to marinate for at least 4 hours, or preferably overnight.

Roast the Pork:

4. Preheat your oven to 350°F (175°C).
5. Remove the marinated pork from the refrigerator and allow it to come to room temperature.
6. Place the marinated pork in a large roasting pan, along with any remaining marinade.
7. Cover the roasting pan with aluminum foil.
8. Roast the pork in the preheated oven for 3-4 hours. After this time, remove the foil and continue roasting for an additional 1-1.5 hours, or until the pork is tender, the skin is crispy, and it reaches an internal temperature of at least 165°F (74°C).

Prepare the Adobo Sauce:

9. While the pork is roasting, prepare the adobo sauce. In a saucepan, heat the vegetable oil over medium heat. Add the finely chopped red onions and sauté until they become soft and translucent.
10. Stir in the achiote oil, ground cumin, dried oregano, salt, and pepper. Cook for a few minutes to infuse the flavors and create a thick sauce. Remove from heat and set aside.

Serve the Hornado:

11. Once the pork is fully roasted and the skin is crispy, remove it

from the oven.
12. Slice the Hornado into portions and drizzle the prepared adobo sauce over the slices or serve it on the side as a dipping sauce.
13. Serve the Hornado hot, accompanied by traditional Ecuadorian sides like llapingachos, mote (hominy), or fried plantains.

Cuy Asado (Roasted Guinea Pig)

Servings: 2-4 **Preparation Time:** 30 minutes **Cooking Time:** 1 hour 30 minutes

Ingredients:
- 2-4 whole guinea pigs (cleaned and prepared, available in some specialty markets)
- 6 cloves garlic, minced
- 2 tablespoons achiote or annatto oil
- 2 tablespoons vegetable oil
- 1 teaspoon ground cumin
- 1 teaspoon dried oregano
- Juice of 2-3 limes or lemons
- Salt and pepper to taste
- 2-4 sprigs of fresh rosemary or thyme (optional, for garnish)

Instructions:

Marinate the Guinea Pigs:
1. Rinse the cleaned and prepared guinea pigs under cold running water and pat them dry with paper towels.
2. In a bowl, combine the minced garlic, achiote or annatto oil, vegetable oil, ground cumin, dried oregano, lime or lemon juice, salt, and pepper. Mix well to create the marinade.
3. Place the guinea pigs in a large dish or baking pan and rub them thoroughly with the marinade, both inside and out. Allow the guinea pigs to marinate for at least 1 hour, or preferably overnight in the refrigerator, covered.

Roast the Guinea Pigs:
4. Preheat your oven to 350°F (175°C).
5. Remove the marinated guinea pigs from the refrigerator and allow them to come to room temperature.
6. Insert a sprig of fresh rosemary or thyme into each guinea pig's cavity, if desired.
7. Place the guinea pigs on a wire rack in a roasting pan to allow for even cooking and air circulation.

8. Roast the guinea pigs in the preheated oven for approximately 1 to 1.5 hours, or until they are golden brown and the meat is cooked through. You can check the doneness by inserting a meat thermometer into the thickest part of the meat; it should read at least 165°F (74°C).
9. Alternatively, you can grill the guinea pigs over medium heat on a barbecue grill for a smoky flavor. Grill for approximately 1 to 1.5 hours, turning occasionally until the skin is crispy and the meat is cooked through.

Serve Cuy Asado:
10. Once the guinea pigs are fully roasted and have a crispy skin, remove them from the oven or grill.
11. Allow them to rest for a few minutes before serving.
12. Serve each roasted guinea pig as a whole, with traditional Ecuadorian sides like boiled potatoes, corn on the cob, or llapingachos, and garnish with lime or lemon wedges.

Note: Guinea pig is a traditional delicacy in Ecuador, especially in the Andean regions. It's important to source guinea pigs from reputable suppliers and ensure they are properly cleaned and prepared before cooking. If you're unfamiliar with cooking guinea pig, consider seeking guidance or assistance from someone experienced in preparing this dish.

Cazuela de Mariscos (Seafood Casserole)

Servings: 4-6 **Preparation Time:** 30 minutes **Cooking Time:** 30 minutes

Ingredients:
For the Seafood:
- 1 pound large shrimp, peeled and deveined
- 1 pound white fish fillets (such as snapper or cod), cut into chunks
- 1/2 pound mussels, cleaned and debearded
- 1/2 pound clams, cleaned
- 1/2 pound calamari rings and tentacles, cleaned and sliced into rings
- 1/2 pound bay scallops (optional)
- 1/2 cup white wine
- Juice of 2-3 limes or lemons
- Salt and pepper to taste

For the Cazuela:
- 2 tablespoons vegetable oil
- 1 onion, finely chopped
- 2 cloves garlic, minced
- 1 bell pepper (red or green), diced
- 1 tomato, finely chopped
- 1/2 cup tomato sauce
- 1/2 teaspoon ground cumin
- 1/2 teaspoon paprika
- 1/4 teaspoon cayenne pepper (adjust to your spice preference)
- 2 cups fish or seafood broth
- 1 cup coconut milk
- Salt and pepper to taste
- Fresh cilantro leaves, chopped (for garnish)
- Lime or lemon wedges (for serving)

Instructions:

Prepare the Seafood:

1. In a bowl, combine the shrimp, white fish chunks, mussels, clams, calamari rings and tentacles, and bay scallops (if using).
2. Pour the white wine and lime or lemon juice over the seafood. Season with salt and pepper to taste. Toss to coat the seafood in the marinade. Allow it to marinate for about 15-20 minutes while you prepare the cazuela.

Prepare the Cazuela:

3. In a large cazuela or deep skillet, heat the vegetable oil over medium-high heat.
4. Add the finely chopped onion and sauté until it becomes soft and translucent.
5. Stir in the minced garlic and cook for an additional minute until fragrant.
6. Add the diced bell pepper and finely chopped tomato. Cook for a few minutes until they start to soften.
7. Pour in the tomato sauce, ground cumin, paprika, and cayenne pepper. Stir to combine the ingredients and create a flavorful base.
8. Pour in the fish or seafood broth and coconut milk. Stir well to incorporate all the flavors.
9. Season the cazuela with salt and pepper to taste. Adjust the seasoning according to your preference.

Cook the Seafood:
10. Carefully add the marinated seafood to the cazuela. Arrange it evenly in the liquid.
11. Cover the cazuela and simmer for about 10-15 minutes, or until the seafood is cooked through, the mussels and clams have opened, and the flavors have melded together. Discard any mussels or clams that do not open.

Serve Cazuela de Mariscos:
12. Garnish the cazuela with chopped fresh cilantro leaves.
13. Serve the Cazuela de Mariscos hot, accompanied by lime or lemon wedges. Offer additional salt and pepper for seasoning at the table.

SIDE DISHES

Tostones (Fried Green Plantains)

Servings: 4-6 **Preparation Time:** 15 minutes **Cooking Time:** 15 minutes

Ingredients:
- 4 green plantains, peeled and cut into 1-inch-thick rounds
- Vegetable oil, for frying
- Salt, to taste
- Dipping sauce (see optional sauce recipes below)

Instructions:

Prepare the Plantains:
1. Start by peeling the green plantains. Slice off the ends, make a lengthwise cut along the ridges, and carefully remove the peel.
2. Cut the peeled plantains into rounds, about 1 inch thick.

First Fry:
3. In a large skillet or frying pan, heat enough vegetable oil over medium-high heat to submerge the plantain rounds.
4. Carefully place the plantain rounds in the hot oil. Fry them for about 2-3 minutes on each side, or until they become golden brown and have softened slightly.
5. Remove the fried plantain rounds from the oil and place them on a paper towel-lined plate to drain excess oil.

Smash the Plantains:
6. Place each fried plantain round between two sheets of plastic

wrap or parchment paper. Using the bottom of a glass or a flat surface, gently press down on the plantain rounds to flatten them to about half their original thickness. They should resemble thick discs.

Second Fry:
7. Return the flattened plantain rounds to the hot oil and fry them for an additional 2-3 minutes on each side, or until they are crispy and golden brown.
8. Remove the tostones from the oil and place them back on the paper towel-lined plate.

Season and Serve:
9. While the tostones are still hot, sprinkle them with salt to taste.
10. Serve the tostones hot and crispy as a side dish or snack. They pair wonderfully with a variety of dipping sauces.

Optional Dipping Sauce Recipes:
- **Garlic Dipping Sauce:** In a small bowl, combine 1/4 cup of mayonnaise, 2 cloves of minced garlic, and the juice of half a lime or lemon. Mix well and season with salt to taste.
- **Spicy Tomato Dipping Sauce:** In a small saucepan, heat 2 tablespoons of vegetable oil over medium heat. Add 1/2 cup of finely chopped onion and sauté until it becomes soft and translucent. Stir in 1/2 cup of tomato sauce, 1/2 teaspoon of hot sauce (adjust to your spice preference), 1/2 teaspoon of paprika, and salt to taste. Simmer for a few minutes until the sauce thickens slightly.

Yuca al Mojo (Yuca with Garlic Sauce)

Servings: 4-6 **Preparation Time:** 15 minutes **Cooking Time:** 20 minutes

Ingredients:
For the Yuca:
- 2 pounds yuca (cassava), peeled and cut into 2-inch-long pieces
- Water, for boiling
- Salt, to taste

For the Mojo Sauce:
- 6 cloves garlic, minced
- 1/2 cup extra-virgin olive oil
- Juice of 2-3 limes or lemons
- Salt and pepper to taste

- Fresh cilantro leaves, chopped (for garnish, optional)

Instructions:

Prepare the Yuca:

1. Start by peeling the yuca (cassava) using a knife. Cut the yuca into 2-inch-long pieces.
2. Fill a large pot with water, add salt to taste, and bring it to a boil.
3. Carefully add the yuca pieces to the boiling water. Boil the yuca for about 15-20 minutes, or until it becomes tender when pierced with a fork.
4. Drain the cooked yuca and set it aside.

Prepare the Mojo Sauce:

5. In a small saucepan, heat the extra-virgin olive oil over low heat.
6. Add the minced garlic to the warm oil and sauté gently for about 2-3 minutes, stirring frequently. Be careful not to brown the garlic; you want it to become aromatic and soften without turning brown.
7. Remove the saucepan from the heat and let it cool slightly.
8. Stir in the lime or lemon juice and season the mojo sauce with salt and pepper to taste. Adjust the acidity and seasoning according to your preference.

Serve Yuca al Mojo:

9. Place the boiled yuca pieces on a serving platter.
10. Drizzle the prepared mojo sauce generously over the yuca.
11. Optionally, garnish with chopped fresh cilantro leaves for a burst of freshness and color.
12. Serve Yuca al Mojo hot as a side dish or appetizer. It's often enjoyed with grilled meats or seafood, making it a delightful complement to a variety of main courses.

Arroz con Coco (Coconut Rice)

Servings: 4-6 **Preparation Time:** 10 minutes **Cooking Time:** 30 minutes

Ingredients:

- 2 cups long-grain white rice
- 1 1/2 cups coconut milk
- 1 1/2 cups water
- 1/4 cup vegetable oil or coconut oil
- 1/2 cup finely grated coconut (fresh or desiccated)
- 1/2 teaspoon salt

- 1/4 cup chopped fresh cilantro or parsley (for garnish, optional)

Instructions:

Rinse the Rice:
1. Place the rice in a fine-mesh strainer and rinse it under cold running water until the water runs clear. Drain the rice and set it aside.

Cook the Rice:
2. In a large saucepan or pot, heat the vegetable oil over medium-high heat.
3. Add the drained rice to the hot oil. Stir and sauté the rice for about 2-3 minutes until it becomes translucent.
4. Pour in the coconut milk and water. Stir well to combine.
5. Add the finely grated coconut and salt to the pot. Stir to incorporate all the ingredients.
6. Bring the mixture to a boil, then reduce the heat to low.
7. Cover the pot with a tight-fitting lid and simmer for about 15-20 minutes, or until the liquid is absorbed and the rice is tender.

Fluff and Serve:
8. Once the rice is cooked, remove the pot from the heat and let it sit, covered, for about 5 minutes to allow the rice to steam.
9. Use a fork to fluff the Arroz con Coco, separating the grains.

Garnish and Enjoy:
10. If desired, garnish the coconut rice with chopped fresh cilantro or parsley before serving.
11. Serve Arroz con Coco hot as a side dish or as a base for your favorite Ecuadorian stews, seafood, or grilled meats.

Mote Pillo (Hominy Corn with Scrambled Eggs)

Servings: 4-6 **Preparation Time:** 15 minutes **Cooking Time:** 20 minutes

Ingredients:
- 2 cups mote (hominy corn), cooked and drained
- 4-6 large eggs
- 1 onion, finely chopped
- 2 cloves garlic, minced
- 2 tablespoons vegetable oil
- Salt and pepper to taste

- Fresh cilantro leaves, chopped (for garnish, optional)

Instructions:

Prepare the Mote:
1. Start by cooking the mote (hominy corn) according to the package instructions. This typically involves simmering it in water until it becomes tender, which can take about 1-2 hours. Drain the cooked mote and set it aside.

Scramble the Eggs:
2. In a large skillet or frying pan, heat the vegetable oil over medium-high heat.
3. Add the finely chopped onion and sauté until it becomes soft and translucent.
4. Stir in the minced garlic and cook for an additional minute until fragrant.
5. Crack the eggs into the skillet and quickly scramble them with a spatula. Continue stirring until the eggs are fully cooked but still moist.

Combine Mote and Eggs:
6. Add the cooked and drained mote (hominy corn) to the skillet with the scrambled eggs.
7. Stir well to combine all the ingredients.
8. Season the mixture with salt and pepper to taste. Adjust the seasoning according to your preference.

Serve Mote Pillo:
9. Optionally, garnish the Mote Pillo with chopped fresh cilantro leaves for added freshness and color.
10. Serve Mote Pillo hot as a hearty breakfast or as a satisfying side dish for lunch or dinner.

Menestra de Lentejas (Lentil Stew)

Servings: 4-6 **Preparation Time:** 15 minutes **Cooking Time:** 45 minutes

Ingredients:
- 2 cups dried green or brown lentils, rinsed and drained
- 6 cups water
- 2 tablespoons vegetable oil
- 1 onion, finely chopped
- 2 cloves garlic, minced
- 1 bell pepper (red or green), diced

- 2 tomatoes, finely chopped
- 1 carrot, diced
- 1/2 cup green peas (fresh or frozen)
- 1/2 teaspoon ground cumin
- 1/2 teaspoon paprika
- 1/4 teaspoon cayenne pepper (adjust to your spice preference)
- Salt and pepper to taste
- Fresh cilantro leaves, chopped (for garnish, optional)
- Lime or lemon wedges (for serving, optional)

Instructions:
Cook the Lentils:
1. Place the rinsed and drained lentils in a large pot. Add 6 cups of water.
2. Bring the water to a boil over high heat, then reduce the heat to low and simmer the lentils for about 25-30 minutes, or until they become tender but not mushy. Drain the cooked lentils and set them aside.

Prepare the Stew:
3. In the same pot, heat the vegetable oil over medium-high heat.
4. Add the finely chopped onion and sauté until it becomes soft and translucent.
5. Stir in the minced garlic and cook for an additional minute until fragrant.
6. Add the diced bell pepper, finely chopped tomatoes, and diced carrot to the pot. Cook for a few minutes until the vegetables start to soften.
7. Season the mixture with ground cumin, paprika, and cayenne pepper. Stir well to coat the vegetables with the spices.

Combine Lentils and Vegetables:
8. Return the cooked lentils to the pot with the sautéed vegetables.
9. Add the green peas (fresh or frozen) to the pot as well.
10. Stir all the ingredients together, ensuring that the lentils and vegetables are well combined.
11. Season the Menestra de Lentejas with salt and pepper to taste. Adjust the seasoning according to your preference.

Simmer and Serve:
12. Cover the pot and simmer the lentil stew for an additional 10-15 minutes to allow the flavors to meld together.
13. Optionally, garnish the Menestra de Lentejas with chopped fresh

cilantro leaves.
14. Serve the lentil stew hot with lime or lemon wedges on the side, if desired.

Espinacas a la Crema (Creamed Spinach)

Servings: 4-6 **Preparation Time:** 10 minutes **Cooking Time:** 20 minutes

Ingredients:
- 2 pounds fresh spinach, washed and trimmed
- 2 tablespoons butter
- 1 small onion, finely chopped
- 2 cloves garlic, minced
- 1 cup heavy cream
- 1/2 cup grated queso fresco or Parmesan cheese
- 1/4 teaspoon ground nutmeg
- Salt and pepper to taste
- Fresh cilantro leaves, chopped (for garnish, optional)

Instructions:

Cook the Spinach:
1. Start by blanching the fresh spinach. Bring a large pot of water to a boil.
2. Carefully add the washed and trimmed spinach to the boiling water. Blanch it for about 1-2 minutes, just until it wilts and becomes bright green.
3. Quickly drain the blanched spinach and transfer it to a bowl of ice water to stop the cooking process. Drain the spinach again and set it aside.

Prepare the Creamed Spinach:
4. In a large skillet or frying pan, melt the butter over medium heat.
5. Add the finely chopped onion and sauté until it becomes soft and translucent.
6. Stir in the minced garlic and cook for an additional minute until fragrant.
7. Pour in the heavy cream and bring it to a gentle simmer. Cook for about 3-4 minutes, allowing the cream to thicken slightly.
8. Add the grated queso fresco or Parmesan cheese to the cream sauce. Stir until the cheese is fully melted and the sauce is smooth.
9. Season the sauce with ground nutmeg, salt, and pepper to taste.

Adjust the seasoning according to your preference.
10. Add the blanched spinach to the cream sauce and toss to coat the spinach with the sauce. Cook for an additional 2-3 minutes, allowing the spinach to heat through.

Serve Espinacas a la Crema:
11. Optionally, garnish the Espinacas a la Crema with chopped fresh cilantro leaves for added freshness and color.
12. Serve the creamed spinach hot as a delicious side dish or as a bed for grilled meats or seafood.

VEGETARIAN AND VEGAN

Ensalada de Palmito (Hearts of Palm Salad)

Servings: 4-6 **Preparation Time:** 15 minutes **Cooking Time:** 0 minutes

Ingredients:
For the Salad:
- 1 can (14 ounces) hearts of palm, drained and sliced into rounds
- 1 red bell pepper, thinly sliced
- 1 red onion, thinly sliced
- 1 cup cherry tomatoes, halved
- 1/4 cup fresh cilantro or parsley leaves, chopped (for garnish, optional)

For the Dressing:
- 3 tablespoons extra-virgin olive oil
- 2 tablespoons white wine vinegar or apple cider vinegar
- 1 clove garlic, minced
- 1 teaspoon Dijon mustard
- Salt and pepper to taste

Instructions:
Prepare the Salad:
1. In a large salad bowl, combine the sliced hearts of palm, thinly sliced red bell pepper, thinly sliced red onion, and halved cherry tomatoes.

Make the Dressing:

2. In a small bowl, whisk together the extra-virgin olive oil, white wine vinegar or apple cider vinegar, minced garlic, Dijon mustard, salt, and pepper. Mix until the dressing is well combined.

Combine Salad and Dressing:
3. Drizzle the dressing over the salad ingredients in the large salad bowl.
4. Gently toss the salad to coat all the ingredients with the dressing.

Garnish and Serve:
5. Optionally, garnish the Ensalada de Palmito with fresh cilantro or parsley leaves for added freshness and color.
6. Serve the Hearts of Palm Salad immediately as a refreshing appetizer or side dish.

Choclo con Queso (Corn with Cheese)

Servings: 4-6 **Preparation Time:** 10 minutes **Cooking Time:** 10 minutes

Ingredients:
- 4-6 ears of fresh corn, husked and cleaned
- 1 cup fresh white cheese (queso fresco) or feta cheese, crumbled
- 1/2 cup grated Parmesan cheese
- 4-6 tablespoons mayonnaise
- 4-6 tablespoons aji sauce (Ecuadorian hot sauce, adjust to your spice preference)
- Fresh cilantro leaves, chopped (for garnish, optional)

Instructions:

Prepare the Corn:
1. Husk and clean the fresh ears of corn, removing any silk.
2. If the corn cobs are long, cut them in half to create shorter pieces, if desired.

Cook the Corn:
3. In a large pot, bring water to a boil. Add the corn cobs to the boiling water.
4. Boil the corn for about 5-7 minutes, or until it becomes tender but still crisp. Be careful not to overcook it.
5. Drain the boiled corn and set it aside.

Assemble Choclo con Queso:
6. While the corn is still warm, spread a layer of mayonnaise evenly over each corn cob.
7. Sprinkle the crumbled white cheese (queso fresco) or feta cheese

generously over the mayonnaise-covered corn.
8. Next, sprinkle grated Parmesan cheese over the other cheese layer.
9. Optionally, drizzle aji sauce (Ecuadorian hot sauce) over the cheese-topped corn. Adjust the amount to your spice preference.

Garnish and Serve:
10. Optionally, garnish Choclo con Queso with chopped fresh cilantro leaves for added freshness and color.
11. Serve the corn with cheese immediately while it's warm.

Acelga Guisada (Stewed Swiss Chard)

Servings: 4-6 **Preparation Time:** 15 minutes **Cooking Time:** 20 minutes

Ingredients:
- 1 bunch Swiss chard, washed and chopped (leaves and stems separated)
- 1 onion, finely chopped
- 2 cloves garlic, minced
- 2 tablespoons vegetable oil
- 1 tomato, finely chopped
- 1 bell pepper (red or green), diced
- 1/2 cup vegetable broth
- 1/2 teaspoon ground cumin
- 1/2 teaspoon paprika
- Salt and pepper to taste
- Fresh cilantro leaves, chopped (for garnish, optional)

Instructions:

Prepare the Swiss Chard:
1. Wash the Swiss chard thoroughly. Separate the leaves from the stems. Chop the leaves and stems separately, as they will be cooked at different times.

Sauté the Vegetables:
2. In a large skillet or frying pan, heat the vegetable oil over medium-high heat.
3. Add the finely chopped onion and sauté until it becomes soft and translucent.
4. Stir in the minced garlic and cook for an additional minute until fragrant.
5. Add the diced bell pepper and chopped Swiss chard stems to the

skillet. Sauté for a few minutes until the stems begin to soften.

Stew the Swiss Chard:

6. Add the chopped Swiss chard leaves and finely chopped tomato to the skillet. Continue cooking for another 2-3 minutes until the leaves wilt.
7. Pour in the vegetable broth to the skillet. Stir well to combine all the ingredients.
8. Season the mixture with ground cumin, paprika, salt, and pepper to taste. Adjust the seasoning according to your preference.
9. Cover the skillet and simmer the Acelga Guisada for about 10-15 minutes, or until the Swiss chard is tender and the flavors have melded together.

Garnish and Serve:

10. Optionally, garnish the stew with chopped fresh cilantro leaves for added freshness and color.
11. Serve Acelga Guisada hot as a delightful and nutritious side dish or as a light vegetarian main course.

Espagueti con Salsa de Maní (Peanut Sauce Pasta)

Servings: 4-6 **Preparation Time:** 10 minutes **Cooking Time:** 15 minutes

Ingredients:
- 12 ounces spaghetti or pasta of your choice
- 1 cup creamy peanut butter
- 1/2 cup vegetable broth
- 1/4 cup soy sauce
- 2 tablespoons vegetable oil
- 1 tablespoon sesame oil
- 2 cloves garlic, minced
- 1 teaspoon grated fresh ginger
- 1/4 cup fresh cilantro leaves, chopped (for garnish)
- Crushed red pepper flakes (for garnish, optional)

Instructions:

Cook the Pasta:

1. Bring a large pot of salted water to a boil. Cook the spaghetti or pasta according to the package instructions until it is al dente. Drain and set aside.

Prepare the Peanut Sauce:
2. In a bowl, whisk together the creamy peanut butter, vegetable broth, soy sauce, vegetable oil, sesame oil, minced garlic, and grated fresh ginger until you have a smooth and creamy peanut sauce. You can adjust the consistency by adding more vegetable broth if needed.

Combine Pasta and Peanut Sauce:
3. Return the cooked and drained pasta to the pot you used to cook it.
4. Pour the peanut sauce over the pasta and toss to coat the pasta evenly with the sauce.

Serve Espagueti con Salsa de Maní:
5. Optionally, garnish with chopped fresh cilantro leaves and a pinch of crushed red pepper flakes for added flavor and color.
6. Serve Espagueti con Salsa de Maní hot as a satisfying and flavorful Ecuadorian-inspired pasta dish.

Ensalada de Frutas (Fruit Salad)

Servings: 4-6 **Preparation Time:** 15 minutes

Ingredients:
- 2 cups fresh pineapple chunks
- 1 cup fresh mango chunks
- 1 cup fresh papaya chunks
- 1 cup fresh strawberries, hulled and halved
- 1 cup fresh blueberries
- 1 cup fresh kiwi chunks
- 1/4 cup fresh mint leaves, chopped (for garnish, optional)
- 1-2 tablespoons honey or agave syrup (optional, for drizzling)
- Juice of 1 lime or lemon

Instructions:

Prepare the Fruits:
1. Wash, peel, and chop the fresh pineapple, mango, papaya, strawberries, blueberries, and kiwi as needed. Ensure that the fruits are ripe and at their peak of freshness.

Combine the Fruits:
2. In a large salad bowl, combine all the prepared fruits.
3. Squeeze the juice of 1 lime or lemon over the fruits. This citrus juice not only adds a zesty flavor but also helps to preserve the freshness of the salad.

Garnish and Serve:
4. Optionally, garnish the Ensalada de Frutas with chopped fresh mint leaves for added freshness and aroma.
5. If you prefer a slightly sweeter salad, drizzle honey or agave syrup over the fruits. Adjust the sweetness according to your preference.
6. Gently toss the fruit salad to combine all the flavors.
7. Serve the Ensalada de Frutas immediately as a refreshing and healthy dessert or side dish.

Arroz con Champiñones (Mushroom Rice)

Servings: 4-6 **Preparation Time:** 10 minutes **Cooking Time:** 25 minutes

Ingredients:
- 2 cups long-grain white rice
- 4 cups vegetable broth
- 2 tablespoons vegetable oil
- 1 onion, finely chopped
- 2 cloves garlic, minced
- 8 ounces button mushrooms, sliced
- 1 cup frozen peas (thawed) or fresh peas
- 1/2 teaspoon ground cumin
- 1/2 teaspoon paprika
- Salt and pepper to taste
- Fresh parsley leaves, chopped (for garnish, optional)

Instructions:

Rinse the Rice:
1. Place the rice in a fine-mesh strainer and rinse it under cold running water until the water runs clear. Drain the rice and set it aside.

Sauté the Mushrooms:
2. In a large skillet or frying pan, heat the vegetable oil over medium-high heat.
3. Add the finely chopped onion and sauté until it becomes soft and translucent.
4. Stir in the minced garlic and cook for an additional minute until fragrant.
5. Add the sliced button mushrooms to the skillet. Sauté for about 5-7 minutes, or until they release their moisture and start to

brown.

Cook the Rice:

6. Add the rinsed and drained rice to the skillet with the sautéed mushrooms. Stir to coat the rice with the mushroom mixture.
7. Pour in the vegetable broth and bring the mixture to a boil.
8. Reduce the heat to low, cover the skillet with a tight-fitting lid, and simmer for about 15-20 minutes, or until the rice is cooked and has absorbed the liquid.

Add Peas and Seasoning:

9. When the rice is almost done, add the thawed frozen peas or fresh peas to the skillet. Stir them into the rice.
10. Season the Mushroom Rice with ground cumin, paprika, salt, and pepper to taste. Adjust the seasoning according to your preference.

Garnish and Serve:

11. Optionally, garnish the Arroz con Champiñones with chopped fresh parsley leaves for added freshness and color.
12. Serve the mushroom rice hot as a satisfying and flavorful Ecuadorian-inspired side dish.

SEAFOOD

Corviche (Fish and Peanut Patties)

Servings: 4-6 **Preparation Time:** 30 minutes **Cooking Time:** 15 minutes

Ingredients:

For the Filling:
- 1 pound white fish fillets (such as cod or hake), finely chopped
- 1 onion, finely chopped
- 2 cloves garlic, minced
- 1 bell pepper (red or green), finely chopped
- 2 tablespoons vegetable oil
- 1/4 cup tomato sauce
- 1 teaspoon ground cumin
- 1 teaspoon ground achiote (annatto) or paprika
- Salt and pepper to taste
- Fresh cilantro leaves, chopped (for garnish, optional)

For the Peanut Dough:
- 2 cups finely ground unsalted peanuts
- 1 cup cornstarch
- 1/4 cup vegetable oil
- 1/2 cup water
- 1 teaspoon salt
- 1/2 teaspoon ground cumin
- 1/2 teaspoon baking powder

For Assembling and Frying:
- Banana leaves, cut into 8x8-inch squares and softened by passing over a flame or in hot water
- Vegetable oil for frying

Instructions:

Prepare the Filling:
1. In a large skillet or frying pan, heat the vegetable oil over medium-high heat.
2. Add the finely chopped onion and sauté until it becomes soft and translucent.
3. Stir in the minced garlic and cook for an additional minute until fragrant.
4. Add the finely chopped bell pepper to the skillet. Sauté for a few minutes until it starts to soften.
5. Add the finely chopped fish to the skillet and cook until it turns opaque.
6. Stir in the tomato sauce, ground cumin, ground achiote (or paprika), salt, and pepper. Cook for a few more minutes until the filling is well seasoned and the flavors meld together. Remove the skillet from heat.

Prepare the Peanut Dough:
7. In a large mixing bowl, combine the finely ground peanuts, cornstarch, vegetable oil, water, salt, ground cumin, and baking powder. Mix well to form a smooth, pliable dough.

Assemble the Corviche:
8. Place a softened banana leaf square on a clean surface.
9. Take a golf ball-sized portion of the peanut dough and flatten it in the center of the banana leaf.
10. Add a spoonful of the fish and vegetable filling on top of the peanut dough.
11. Carefully fold the banana leaf over the filling to form a square or rectangular package, sealing the edges. You can use twine or toothpicks to secure the corviche, if needed.

Fry the Corviche:
12. In a large frying pan, heat vegetable oil over medium-high heat.
13. Carefully place the assembled corviche packages, seam-side down, in the hot oil.
14. Fry the corviche for about 3-4 minutes on each side, or until they turn golden brown and crispy.

15. Remove the fried corviche from the oil and drain on paper towels to remove excess oil.

Serve Corviche:
16. Optionally, garnish the Corviche with chopped fresh cilantro leaves for added freshness and aroma.
17. Serve the Corviche hot as a delightful Ecuadorian coastal snack or appetizer.

Camarones al Ajillo (Garlic Shrimp)

Servings: 4-6 **Preparation Time:** 10 minutes **Cooking Time:** 10 minutes

Ingredients:
- 1 1/2 pounds large shrimp, peeled and deveined
- 6 cloves garlic, minced
- 1/4 cup fresh parsley leaves, chopped
- 1/4 cup white wine (optional)
- 3 tablespoons olive oil
- 2 tablespoons butter
- 1/4 teaspoon red pepper flakes (adjust to your spice preference)
- Salt and black pepper to taste
- Juice of 1 lemon
- Lemon wedges (for garnish, optional)

Instructions:

Prepare the Shrimp:
1. Ensure the shrimp are peeled and deveined, leaving the tails on for presentation.

Sauté the Shrimp:
2. In a large skillet or frying pan, heat the olive oil and butter over medium-high heat.
3. Add the minced garlic and red pepper flakes to the skillet. Sauté for about 1 minute until the garlic becomes fragrant.
4. Add the shrimp to the skillet in a single layer, making sure not to overcrowd the pan. Cook for about 2-3 minutes on each side, or until the shrimp turn pink and opaque.

Deglaze with Wine (Optional):
5. If using white wine, pour it into the skillet and stir to deglaze the pan, scraping up any browned bits. Allow the wine to simmer for about 1-2 minutes to reduce slightly.

Season and Finish:

6. Season the Camarones al Ajillo with salt and black pepper to taste. Adjust the seasoning according to your preference.
7. Squeeze the juice of 1 lemon over the shrimp and sprinkle the chopped fresh parsley on top.

Garnish and Serve:

8. Optionally, garnish the garlic shrimp with lemon wedges for extra zesty flavor and presentation.
9. Serve the Camarones al Ajillo hot as an appetizer or main course.

Pescado Encocado (Fish in Coconut Sauce)

Servings: 4-6 **Preparation Time:** 15 minutes **Cooking Time:** 30 minutes

Ingredients:

For the Fish:
- 1 1/2 pounds white fish fillets (such as snapper or sea bass), cut into serving-size pieces
- Juice of 1 lime
- Salt and pepper to taste

For the Coconut Sauce:
- 2 tablespoons vegetable oil
- 1 onion, finely chopped
- 2 cloves garlic, minced
- 1 red bell pepper, finely chopped
- 1 green bell pepper, finely chopped
- 2 tomatoes, finely chopped
- 1/2 teaspoon ground cumin
- 1/2 teaspoon ground achiote (annatto) or paprika
- 1 can (14 ounces) coconut milk
- Salt and pepper to taste
- Fresh cilantro leaves, chopped (for garnish, optional)

Instructions:

Marinate the Fish:

1. Place the fish pieces in a bowl and squeeze the juice of 1 lime over them. Season with salt and pepper to taste. Let the fish marinate while you prepare the coconut sauce.

Prepare the Coconut Sauce:

2. In a large skillet or frying pan, heat the vegetable oil over medium-high heat.
3. Add the finely chopped onion and sauté until it becomes soft and

translucent.
4. Stir in the minced garlic and cook for an additional minute until fragrant.
5. Add the finely chopped red and green bell peppers to the skillet. Sauté for a few minutes until they start to soften.
6. Add the finely chopped tomatoes to the skillet and cook for about 3-5 minutes until they break down and become somewhat saucy.
7. Stir in the ground cumin and ground achiote (or paprika) to the mixture.
8. Pour in the can of coconut milk, and season with salt and pepper to taste. Stir well to combine all the ingredients.
9. Allow the coconut sauce to simmer for about 10-15 minutes, or until it thickens and the flavors meld together.

Cook the Fish:
10. While the coconut sauce is simmering, remove the fish from the marinade and pat it dry with paper towels.
11. In a separate skillet, heat a bit of vegetable oil over medium-high heat.
12. Pan-sear the fish pieces for about 2-3 minutes on each side, or until they turn golden brown and are cooked through. Be careful not to overcook.

Combine Sauce and Fish:
13. Once the coconut sauce has thickened to your liking, gently add the cooked fish pieces to the skillet with the sauce.
14. Let the fish simmer in the coconut sauce for a few minutes to absorb the flavors.

Garnish and Serve:
15. Optionally, garnish Pescado Encocado with chopped fresh cilantro leaves for added freshness and aroma.
16. Serve this delightful Ecuadorian dish hot as a comforting and flavor-packed main course.

Arroz Marinero (Seafood Rice)

Servings: 4-6 **Preparation Time:** 15 minutes **Cooking Time:** 30 minutes

Ingredients:
- 2 cups long-grain white rice
- 4 cups seafood or vegetable broth

ECUADORIAN COOKBOOK

- 1 pound mixed seafood (shrimp, squid, mussels, etc.), cleaned and prepared
- 1 onion, finely chopped
- 2 cloves garlic, minced
- 1 bell pepper (red or green), finely chopped
- 2 tomatoes, finely chopped
- 1/2 cup frozen peas (thawed) or fresh peas
- 1/2 teaspoon ground cumin
- 1/2 teaspoon paprika
- 1/2 teaspoon saffron threads (optional, for color and flavor)
- Salt and pepper to taste
- 2 tablespoons vegetable oil
- Lemon wedges (for garnish, optional)
- Fresh parsley leaves, chopped (for garnish, optional)

Instructions:

Rinse the Rice:

1. Place the rice in a fine-mesh strainer and rinse it under cold running water until the water runs clear. Drain the rice and set it aside.

Prepare the Seafood:

2. Ensure the seafood is cleaned and prepared as needed. You can peel and devein shrimp, clean squid, and scrub mussels, discarding any with broken shells.

Sauté the Aromatics:

3. In a large skillet or paella pan, heat the vegetable oil over medium-high heat.
4. Add the finely chopped onion and sauté until it becomes soft and translucent.
5. Stir in the minced garlic and cook for an additional minute until fragrant.
6. Add the finely chopped bell pepper to the skillet. Sauté for a few minutes until it starts to soften.

Add Tomatoes and Spices:

7. Stir in the finely chopped tomatoes and cook for about 3-5 minutes until they break down and become somewhat saucy.
8. Sprinkle ground cumin, paprika, and saffron threads (if using) over the tomato mixture. Stir to incorporate the spices evenly.

Cook the Rice:

9. Add the rinsed and drained rice to the skillet. Stir to coat the rice

with the tomato and spice mixture.
10. Pour in the seafood or vegetable broth and season with salt and pepper to taste. Stir well to combine all the ingredients.
11. Allow the rice to simmer over medium-low heat for about 15-20 minutes, or until it is almost cooked and most of the liquid has been absorbed. Stir occasionally to prevent sticking.

Add Seafood and Peas:
12. Arrange the prepared seafood and thawed frozen peas (or fresh peas) over the partially cooked rice.
13. Cover the skillet or paella pan with a lid or aluminum foil and let the seafood and rice simmer for an additional 10-15 minutes, or until the seafood is cooked through and the rice is tender.

Garnish and Serve:
14. Optionally, garnish Arroz Marinero with lemon wedges and chopped fresh parsley leaves for added flavor and presentation.
15. Serve this exquisite Ecuadorian seafood rice hot as a main course.

Encocado de Camarones (Shrimp in Coconut Sauce)

Servings: 4-6 **Preparation Time:** 15 minutes **Cooking Time:** 20 minutes

Ingredients:
For the Shrimp:
- 1 1/2 pounds large shrimp, peeled and deveined
- Juice of 1 lime
- Salt and pepper to taste

For the Coconut Sauce:
- 2 tablespoons vegetable oil
- 1 onion, finely chopped
- 2 cloves garlic, minced
- 1 red bell pepper, finely chopped
- 1 green bell pepper, finely chopped
- 2 tomatoes, finely chopped
- 1 can (14 ounces) coconut milk
- 1/2 cup seafood or vegetable broth
- 1/2 teaspoon ground cumin
- 1/2 teaspoon paprika
- Salt and pepper to taste

- Fresh cilantro leaves, chopped (for garnish, optional)
- Sliced green onions (for garnish, optional)

Instructions:

Marinate the Shrimp:

1. Place the peeled and deveined shrimp in a bowl and squeeze the juice of 1 lime over them. Season with salt and pepper to taste. Let the shrimp marinate while you prepare the coconut sauce.

Prepare the Coconut Sauce:

2. In a large skillet or frying pan, heat the vegetable oil over medium-high heat.
3. Add the finely chopped onion and sauté until it becomes soft and translucent.
4. Stir in the minced garlic and cook for an additional minute until fragrant.
5. Add the finely chopped red and green bell peppers to the skillet. Sauté for a few minutes until they start to soften.
6. Add the finely chopped tomatoes to the skillet and cook for about 3-5 minutes until they break down and become somewhat saucy.
7. Stir in the ground cumin and paprika to the mixture.
8. Pour in the can of coconut milk and seafood or vegetable broth. Season with salt and pepper to taste. Stir well to combine all the ingredients.
9. Allow the coconut sauce to simmer for about 10-15 minutes, or until it thickens and the flavors meld together.

Cook the Shrimp:

10. While the coconut sauce is simmering, remove the shrimp from the marinade and pat them dry with paper towels.
11. In a separate skillet, heat a bit of vegetable oil over medium-high heat.
12. Quickly pan-sear the shrimp for about 2-3 minutes on each side, or until they turn pink and opaque. Be careful not to overcook.

Combine Sauce and Shrimp:

13. Once the coconut sauce has thickened to your liking, gently add the cooked shrimp to the skillet with the sauce.
14. Let the shrimp simmer in the coconut sauce for a few minutes to absorb the flavors.

Garnish and Serve:

15. Optionally, garnish Encocado de Camarones with chopped fresh

cilantro leaves and sliced green onions for added freshness and color.
16. Serve this delightful Ecuadorian dish hot as a flavorful main course.

Ceviche Mixto (Mixed Seafood Ceviche)

Servings: 4-6 **Preparation Time:** 20 minutes **Marinating Time:** 20-30 minutes

Ingredients:
- 1/2 pound fresh white fish fillets (such as sea bass or sole), diced into small pieces
- 1/2 pound fresh shrimp, peeled, deveined, and chopped
- 1/4 pound fresh squid, cleaned and sliced into rings
- Juice of 4-5 limes
- Juice of 2 lemons
- 1 red onion, thinly sliced
- 1-2 hot chili peppers (rocoto, aji amarillo, or jalapeño), finely chopped (adjust to your spice preference)
- 2-3 cloves garlic, minced
- 1 red bell pepper, finely chopped
- 1/4 cup fresh cilantro leaves, chopped
- Salt and pepper to taste
- Corn on the cob or corn nuts (cancha) for serving (optional)
- Sweet potato, boiled and sliced (for serving, optional)
- Lettuce leaves (for serving, optional)
- Chifles (fried plantain chips, for serving, optional)

Instructions:

Prepare the Seafood:
1. Ensure the white fish fillets are diced into small pieces, the shrimp are peeled, deveined, and chopped, and the squid is cleaned and sliced into rings. Pat them dry with paper towels.

Marinate the Seafood:
2. In a large glass or non-reactive bowl, combine the diced fish, chopped shrimp, and sliced squid.
3. Squeeze the juice of limes and lemons over the seafood to cover it completely. Make sure the seafood is fully submerged in the citrus juice. Allow it to marinate for about 20-30 minutes in the refrigerator. The acid in the citrus juice will "cook" the seafood, turning it opaque.

Prepare the Vegetables:
4. While the seafood is marinating, thinly slice the red onion, finely chop the hot chili peppers, mince the garlic, finely chop the red bell pepper, and chop the fresh cilantro leaves.

Assemble the Ceviche:
5. After the seafood has marinated, drain off most of the citrus juice. Leave just enough to keep the ceviche moist but not swimming in juice.
6. Add the sliced red onion, chopped chili peppers (adjust the amount according to your spice preference), minced garlic, chopped red bell pepper, and fresh cilantro to the seafood. Mix everything together gently.
7. Season the Ceviche Mixto with salt and pepper to taste. Adjust the seasoning to your preference.

Serve Ceviche Mixto:
8. Optionally, serve the ceviche on a bed of lettuce leaves, garnished with slices of boiled sweet potato and accompanied by corn on the cob or corn nuts (cancha).
9. Serve with chifles (fried plantain chips) for a delightful textural contrast.

DESSERTS

Tres Leches Cake

Servings: 12-16 **Preparation Time:** 20 minutes **Baking Time:** 30 minutes **Chilling Time:** 4 hours or overnight
Ingredients:
For the Cake:
- 1 1/2 cups all-purpose flour
- 1 1/2 teaspoons baking powder
- 1/2 teaspoon salt
- 1/2 cup unsalted butter, softened
- 1 cup granulated sugar
- 5 large eggs
- 1 teaspoon vanilla extract
- 1/2 cup whole milk

For the Three Milks Mixture:
- 1 can (14 ounces) sweetened condensed milk
- 1 can (12 ounces) evaporated milk
- 1 cup whole milk

For the Topping:
- 2 cups heavy whipping cream
- 1/4 cup powdered sugar
- 1 teaspoon vanilla extract
- Ground cinnamon or cocoa powder for dusting (optional)

Instructions:

Prepare the Cake:

1. Preheat your oven to 350°F (175°C). Grease and flour a 9x13-inch baking dish or cake pan.
2. In a medium-sized bowl, whisk together the all-purpose flour, baking powder, and salt. Set aside.
3. In a large mixing bowl, cream together the softened butter and granulated sugar until light and fluffy, which should take about 3-4 minutes.
4. Add the eggs one at a time, beating well after each addition. Stir in the vanilla extract.
5. Gradually add the dry ingredients to the wet ingredients, mixing until just combined.
6. Stir in the 1/2 cup of whole milk until the cake batter is smooth.
7. Pour the cake batter into the prepared baking dish, spreading it evenly.
8. Bake in the preheated oven for about 30 minutes or until the cake is lightly golden and a toothpick inserted into the center comes out clean.

Prepare the Three Milks Mixture:

9. While the cake is baking, in a separate bowl, combine the sweetened condensed milk, evaporated milk, and 1 cup of whole milk. Mix well.

Assemble and Soak the Cake:

10. Once the cake is out of the oven and still warm, use a fork or skewer to poke holes all over the surface of the cake. This will help the milk mixture soak into the cake.
11. Carefully pour the three milks mixture evenly over the warm cake. Make sure it soaks into the holes.
12. Let the cake cool to room temperature, and then cover it with plastic wrap. Refrigerate for at least 4 hours or, ideally, overnight to allow the cake to absorb the milks.

Prepare the Topping:

13. Before serving, in a mixing bowl, whip the heavy whipping cream, powdered sugar, and vanilla extract until it forms stiff peaks.

Finish and Serve:

14. Spread the whipped cream topping evenly over the chilled Tres Leches Cake.
15. Optionally, dust the top with ground cinnamon or cocoa powder

for a decorative touch.
16. Cut into squares and serve this delectable Ecuadorian dessert.

Arroz con Leche (Rice Pudding)

Servings: 6-8 **Preparation Time:** 10 minutes **Cooking Time:** 30 minutes **Chilling Time:** 2 hours (optional)

Ingredients:
- 1 cup long-grain white rice
- 4 cups whole milk
- 1 cup granulated sugar
- 1 cinnamon stick
- 1 lemon peel (use a vegetable peeler to remove a strip of lemon zest)
- 1/2 teaspoon ground cinnamon (for garnish)
- Ground nutmeg (for garnish, optional)
- Raisins (for garnish, optional)

Instructions:

Prepare the Rice:
1. Rinse the rice thoroughly under cold running water until the water runs clear. Drain the rice.

Cook the Rice:
2. In a large saucepan, combine the rinsed rice, whole milk, granulated sugar, cinnamon stick, and lemon peel.
3. Place the saucepan over medium-high heat and bring the mixture to a boil, stirring occasionally.
4. Reduce the heat to low and let the rice mixture simmer gently. Stir frequently to prevent the rice from sticking to the bottom of the pan.
5. Cook the rice for about 25-30 minutes or until it is tender and the mixture has thickened to a creamy consistency.

Remove the Flavorings:
6. Once the rice is cooked, remove the cinnamon stick and lemon peel from the mixture.

Chill the Rice Pudding (Optional):
7. If you prefer your rice pudding chilled, transfer it to a bowl and cover it with plastic wrap, ensuring the wrap touches the surface of the pudding to prevent a skin from forming. Refrigerate for at least 2 hours or until it's cold.

Serve Arroz con Leche:

8. When ready to serve, spoon the rice pudding into individual serving dishes or bowls.
9. Optionally, sprinkle ground cinnamon and ground nutmeg on top for a touch of spice and flavor.
10. You can also garnish with raisins if desired.
11. Serve this comforting Ecuadorian dessert warm or chilled.

Morocho (Corn Pudding)

Servings: 6-8 **Preparation Time:** 15 minutes **Cooking Time:** 1 hour 15 minutes

Ingredients:
- 1 cup dried morocho corn kernels
- 4 cups whole milk
- 1 cinnamon stick
- 1 cup granulated sugar
- 1/2 teaspoon ground cinnamon (for garnish)
- Ground nutmeg (for garnish, optional)
- Raisins (for garnish, optional)

Instructions:

Prepare the Morocho:
1. Rinse the dried morocho corn kernels thoroughly under cold running water. Drain.
2. In a large bowl, cover the morocho kernels with enough water to submerge them completely. Let them soak overnight or for at least 8 hours. This will soften the corn and make it easier to cook.

Cook the Morocho:
3. After soaking, drain the morocho kernels.
4. In a large saucepan, combine the soaked morocho kernels, whole milk, and cinnamon stick.
5. Place the saucepan over medium-high heat and bring the mixture to a boil, stirring occasionally.
6. Reduce the heat to low and let the morocho simmer gently. Stir frequently to prevent it from sticking to the bottom of the pan.
7. Cook the morocho for about 1 hour or until it becomes tender and the mixture thickens to a pudding-like consistency.

Sweeten the Morocho:
8. Stir in the granulated sugar and continue to cook for an additional 15 minutes, or until the sugar is fully dissolved and the pudding is sweetened to your liking.

ECUADORIAN COOKBOOK

Remove the Flavorings:
9. Once the morocho pudding is cooked and sweetened, remove the cinnamon stick from the mixture.

Serve Morocho:
10. Spoon the morocho pudding into individual serving dishes or bowls.
11. Optionally, sprinkle ground cinnamon and ground nutmeg on top for a touch of spice and flavor.
12. You can also garnish with raisins if desired.
13. Serve Morocho warm as a comforting and traditional Ecuadorian dessert.

Dulce de Higos (Fig Jam)

Servings: Approximately 2 cups **Preparation Time:** 15 minutes **Cooking Time:** 1 hour

Ingredients:
- 2 cups fresh figs, washed and stems removed
- 1 1/2 cups granulated sugar
- 1/2 cup water
- 1 cinnamon stick
- 3 cloves
- 1 lemon, thinly sliced
- 1/2 teaspoon vanilla extract (optional)

Instructions:

Prepare the Figs:
1. Wash the fresh figs thoroughly and remove their stems. You can leave them whole or cut them into halves or quarters, depending on your preference.

Cook the Fig Jam:
2. In a large saucepan, combine the prepared figs, granulated sugar, water, cinnamon stick, and cloves.
3. Place the saucepan over medium-high heat and bring the mixture to a boil, stirring occasionally.
4. Once the mixture reaches a boil, reduce the heat to low and let it simmer gently. Stir occasionally to ensure the sugar is fully dissolved.
5. Cook the figs for about 45 minutes to 1 hour, or until they become soft and the syrup thickens to your desired consistency. You can test the consistency by placing a small amount of the

syrup on a cold plate; it should thicken as it cools.
6. During the last few minutes of cooking, add the thinly sliced lemon and vanilla extract (if using) to the fig mixture. Stir to incorporate these flavors.

Remove Flavorings and Cool:
7. Once the fig jam is cooked to your liking, remove the cinnamon stick and cloves from the mixture.

Store or Serve:
8. You can transfer the hot fig jam into sterilized jars while it's still hot for long-term storage. Seal the jars tightly and store them in a cool, dark place. Properly sealed jars can be stored for several months.
9. Alternatively, let the fig jam cool to room temperature before transferring it to a clean container with a tight-fitting lid if you plan to consume it within a shorter time frame.

Enjoy Dulce de Higos:
10. Serve Dulce de Higos as a sweet and fruity topping for bread, crackers, or cheese. It's also a delightful accompaniment to desserts or a delicious addition to your morning toast or yogurt.

Cocadas (Coconut Candies)

Servings: Approximately 24 cocadas **Preparation Time:** 15 minutes **Cooking Time:** 20 minutes

Ingredients:
- 3 cups shredded sweetened coconut
- 1 cup granulated sugar
- 1/2 cup water
- 1/4 cup unsalted butter
- 1/4 teaspoon salt
- 1 teaspoon vanilla extract
- 2 large egg whites

Instructions:

Prepare the Baking Sheet:
1. Line a baking sheet with parchment paper or use a silicone baking mat. This will prevent the cocadas from sticking to the sheet.

Combine Ingredients:
2. In a large saucepan, combine the granulated sugar, water, unsalted butter, and salt. Place the saucepan over medium heat and stir until the sugar is fully dissolved.

3. Once the mixture comes to a boil, reduce the heat to low and simmer for about 5 minutes, allowing it to thicken slightly.
4. Stir in the shredded sweetened coconut and continue to cook, stirring constantly, for an additional 5-7 minutes. The mixture should thicken further and become sticky.

Whip the Egg Whites:
5. While the coconut mixture is cooking, in a separate mixing bowl, use an electric mixer to whip the egg whites until they form stiff peaks.

Combine Coconut and Egg Whites:
6. Once the coconut mixture is ready, remove it from the heat and stir in the vanilla extract.
7. Gently fold the whipped egg whites into the coconut mixture until well combined. Be careful not to deflate the egg whites too much; they should provide a light and airy texture to the cocadas.

Shape the Cocadas:
8. Using a spoon or your hands, scoop portions of the coconut mixture and shape them into small rounds or mounds on the prepared baking sheet. You can make them as big or as small as you like, but traditionally, they are bite-sized.

Let Them Cool:
9. Allow the cocadas to cool at room temperature for about 1-2 hours, or until they are firm and set.

Serve Cocadas:
10. Once the cocadas have cooled and hardened, you can remove them from the baking sheet and serve. They are a delightful sweet treat with a chewy coconut texture and a hint of vanilla.
11. Enjoy Cocadas as a traditional Ecuadorian candy, a sweet snack, or a delightful addition to your dessert platter.

Suspiros (Meringue Cookies)

Servings: Approximately 24 meringue cookies **Preparation Time:** 15 minutes **Baking Time:** 1 hour 15 minutes

Ingredients:
- 4 large egg whites, at room temperature
- 1 cup granulated sugar
- 1/2 teaspoon vanilla extract
- A pinch of salt
- Powdered sugar, for dusting (optional)

Instructions:
Preheat the Oven:
1. Preheat your oven to 225°F (110°C). Line two baking sheets with parchment paper or use silicone baking mats.

Whip the Egg Whites:
2. In a clean, dry mixing bowl, add the room temperature egg whites and a pinch of salt.
3. Use an electric mixer on medium-high speed to whip the egg whites until they form soft peaks. This should take about 2-3 minutes.
4. Gradually add the granulated sugar, a spoonful at a time, while continuing to whip the egg whites. Make sure each addition is fully incorporated before adding more sugar.
5. Continue whipping the egg whites until they become glossy and form stiff peaks. This should take another 2-3 minutes.

Add Vanilla Extract:
6. Gently fold in the vanilla extract until it's evenly incorporated into the meringue.

Pipe the Meringue:
7. You can pipe the meringue cookies onto the prepared baking sheets using a pastry bag and a star or round tip, or simply drop spoonfuls of meringue onto the sheets using a spoon.

Bake the Meringue Cookies:
8. Place the baking sheets in the preheated oven.
9. Bake the meringue cookies for about 1 hour and 15 minutes, or until they are dry and crisp to the touch. The baking time may vary slightly depending on your oven.

Cool and Serve:
10. Once the meringue cookies are baked, remove them from the oven and let them cool completely on the baking sheets. They will become crisp as they cool.
11. Optionally, dust the meringue cookies with powdered sugar just before serving for a decorative touch.
12. Serve Suspiros as a delightful Ecuadorian treat. These light and airy meringue cookies are perfect for satisfying your sweet cravings or for sharing with friends and family.

Higos con Queso (Figs with Cheese)

Servings: 4-6 **Preparation Time:** 10 minutes **Cooking Time:** 5

minutes

Ingredients:
- 8-12 fresh ripe figs
- 4-6 slices of fresh white cheese (queso fresco or queso blanco)
- 1/4 cup honey
- 1/4 cup chopped nuts (such as almonds or walnuts), toasted
- Fresh mint leaves for garnish (optional)

Instructions:

Prepare the Figs:
1. Wash the fresh figs thoroughly and pat them dry with a paper towel.
2. Cut a small "X" into the top of each fig, about halfway down. This will help the figs open up when cooked.

Grill or Pan-Sear the Figs:
3. Heat a grill or grill pan over medium-high heat. If you don't have a grill, you can use a regular pan.
4. Place the figs, cut side down, on the grill or in the pan.
5. Grill or pan-sear the figs for about 2-3 minutes, or until they develop grill marks and become slightly caramelized. Turn them over and cook for another 2-3 minutes on the other side.
6. Remove the figs from the grill or pan and set them aside.

Assemble Higos con Queso:
7. On a serving plate, arrange the grilled figs.
8. Place a slice of fresh white cheese on top of each fig.
9. Drizzle honey over the figs and cheese. You can adjust the amount of honey to your taste.
10. Sprinkle the toasted chopped nuts over the figs and cheese.

Garnish and Serve:
11. Optionally, garnish the dish with fresh mint leaves for a pop of color and added freshness.
12. Serve Higos con Queso immediately as a delightful Ecuadorian dessert or appetizer.

BEVERAGES

Chicha

Ingredients:
- 1 cup dried purple maize (maíz morado)
- 8 cups water
- 2 cinnamon sticks
- 4 cloves
- 1 pineapple, peeled and chopped
- 1 cup brown sugar
- 1 apple, peeled and chopped
- 1 quince, peeled and chopped
- Juice of 4 limes
- Pineapple or apple slices for garnish (optional)

Instructions:

Prepare the Purple Maize:
1. Rinse the dried purple maize under cold running water until the water runs clear. Drain.
2. In a large pot, combine the rinsed maize and 8 cups of water. Add the cinnamon sticks and cloves.
3. Bring the mixture to a boil over medium-high heat.
4. Reduce the heat to low, cover the pot, and let it simmer for about 45 minutes to 1 hour. The maize should become soft, and the liquid will take on a deep purple color. Remove from heat.

Strain and Cool:

ECUADORIAN COOKBOOK

5. Strain the liquid through a fine-mesh sieve or cheesecloth into a clean container, discarding the solid maize and spices.
6. Allow the purple maize liquid to cool to room temperature.

Prepare the Fruit Base:

7. In a blender, combine the chopped pineapple, brown sugar, chopped apple, chopped quince, and lime juice.
8. Blend until you have a smooth fruit mixture.

Combine the Maize Liquid and Fruit Base:

9. Pour the cooled purple maize liquid and the fruit mixture into a large pitcher or container. Stir to combine.
10. Taste the chicha and adjust the sweetness by adding more sugar if desired.
11. Chill the chicha in the refrigerator for at least 1-2 hours to allow the flavors to meld.

Serve Chicha:

12. When ready to serve, pour the chilled chicha into glasses.
13. Optionally, garnish each glass with a slice of pineapple or apple.

Colada Morada

Ingredients:
- 1 cup dried purple maize (maíz morado)
- 8 cups water
- 4 cinnamon sticks
- 6 cloves
- 4 allspice berries
- 4 cups fresh blackberries
- 1 cup fresh blueberries
- 1 cup strawberries, hulled and halved
- 1 cup pineapple chunks
- 1 cup chopped naranjilla or orange segments
- 1 cup chopped babaco or papaya
- 1 cup brown sugar (adjust to taste)
- Juice of 4 limes
- 1 teaspoon grated orange zest
- 1/4 cup dried pineapple or apricots (optional)
- Pineapple or orange slices for garnish (optional)

Instructions:

Prepare the Purple Maize:

1. Rinse the dried purple maize under cold running water until the

water runs clear. Drain.
2. In a large pot, combine the rinsed maize, 8 cups of water, cinnamon sticks, cloves, and allspice berries.
3. Bring the mixture to a boil over medium-high heat.
4. Reduce the heat to low, cover the pot, and let it simmer for about 45 minutes to 1 hour. The maize should become soft, and the liquid will take on a deep purple color. Remove from heat.

Strain and Cool:
5. Strain the liquid through a fine-mesh sieve or cheesecloth into a clean container, discarding the solid maize and spices.
6. Allow the purple maize liquid to cool to room temperature.

Prepare the Fruit:
7. In a blender, combine the fresh blackberries, blueberries, strawberries, pineapple chunks, naranjilla or orange segments, and babaco or papaya. Blend until you have a smooth fruit mixture.

Combine the Maize Liquid and Fruit Puree:
8. Pour the cooled purple maize liquid and the fruit puree into a large pot.
9. Add the brown sugar, lime juice, and grated orange zest. Stir to combine.
10. Taste the colada morada and adjust the sweetness by adding more sugar if desired.

Simmer and Thicken:
11. Place the pot over medium heat and bring the mixture to a gentle simmer.
12. Allow the colada morada to simmer for about 15-20 minutes, stirring occasionally, until it thickens slightly.

Optional Dried Fruits:
13. If you're using dried pineapple or apricots, chop them into small pieces and add them to the colada morada during the last 5 minutes of simmering. They will rehydrate and add a delightful chewy texture.

Serve Colada Morada:
14. When ready to serve, ladle the colada morada into bowls or mugs.
15. Optionally, garnish each serving with a slice of pineapple or orange.
16. Enjoy colada morada as a cherished Ecuadorian beverage, often

enjoyed during Day of the Dead (Día de los Difuntos) celebrations.

Canelazo

Ingredients:
- 2 cups water
- 4 cinnamon sticks
- 4 cloves
- 4 allspice berries
- 1 cup dark brown sugar
- 1 cup aguardiente (or substitute with rum or brandy)
- 1 cup orange juice
- 1/4 cup lime juice
- Orange and lime slices for garnish (optional)
- Cinnamon sticks for garnish (optional)

Instructions:

Prepare the Spiced Infusion:
1. In a medium-sized pot, combine the water, cinnamon sticks, cloves, and allspice berries.
2. Place the pot over medium-high heat and bring the mixture to a boil.
3. Reduce the heat to low, cover the pot, and let it simmer for about 20-25 minutes. This will infuse the water with the warm spices.
4. After simmering, remove the pot from heat and strain the spiced infusion into a clean container, discarding the spices.

Prepare the Canelazo:
5. Return the spiced infusion to the pot.
6. Stir in the dark brown sugar until it dissolves completely.
7. Place the pot back over low heat and continue to heat the mixture, stirring, until it's hot but not boiling.
8. Remove the pot from the heat and stir in the aguardiente, rum, or brandy.
9. Add the orange juice and lime juice and stir to combine.

Serve Canelazo:
10. Ladle the canelazo into mugs or heatproof glasses.
11. Optionally, garnish each mug with a slice of orange and lime, and add a cinnamon stick for extra flavor and decoration.
12. Serve canelazo as a comforting and warming Ecuadorian beverage, especially during the colder months.

Jugo de Maracuyá (Passion Fruit Juice)

Ingredients:
- 6 ripe passion fruits
- 2 cups water
- 1/4 cup granulated sugar (adjust to taste)
- Ice cubes (optional)
- Fresh mint leaves for garnish (optional)

Instructions:

Prepare the Passion Fruits:
1. Wash the passion fruits thoroughly under cold running water.
2. Cut each passion fruit in half.
3. Scoop out the pulp and seeds into a blender or a bowl. You can use a spoon to help with this process.

Blend the Passion Fruit Pulp:
4. In a blender, combine the passion fruit pulp and seeds with 2 cups of water.
5. Blend the mixture for a few seconds until it's well combined, but be careful not to over-blend, as you want to avoid breaking the seeds, which can make the juice bitter.

Strain the Juice:
6. Strain the passion fruit juice through a fine-mesh sieve or cheesecloth into a clean container to remove any remaining seeds. You can use a spoon to gently press the pulp to extract more juice.

Sweeten the Juice:
7. Taste the passion fruit juice and add granulated sugar to sweeten it to your liking. Stir until the sugar is fully dissolved.
8. You can adjust the sweetness by adding more sugar if needed.

Chill the Juice:
9. If desired, refrigerate the passion fruit juice for about 30 minutes to chill it. Alternatively, you can serve it immediately over ice cubes for a refreshing cold drink.

Serve Jugo de Maracuyá:
10. Pour the passion fruit juice into glasses.
11. Optionally, garnish each glass with a sprig of fresh mint for added freshness.

Jugo de Tomate de Árbol (Tree Tomato Juice)

Ingredients:
- 6 ripe tree tomatoes (tomates de árbol)
- 2 cups water
- 1/4 cup granulated sugar (adjust to taste)
- Ice cubes (optional)
- Fresh mint leaves for garnish (optional)

Instructions:

Prepare the Tree Tomatoes:
1. Wash the tree tomatoes thoroughly under cold running water.
2. Cut each tree tomato in half.
3. Scoop out the pulp and seeds into a blender or a bowl. You can use a spoon to help with this process.

Blend the Tree Tomato Pulp:
4. In a blender, combine the tree tomato pulp with 2 cups of water.
5. Blend the mixture for a few seconds until it's well combined.

Strain the Juice:
6. Strain the tree tomato juice through a fine-mesh sieve or cheesecloth into a clean container to remove any remaining seeds or pulp.

Sweeten the Juice:
7. Taste the tree tomato juice and add granulated sugar to sweeten it to your liking. Stir until the sugar is fully dissolved.
8. You can adjust the sweetness by adding more sugar if needed.

Chill the Juice:
9. If desired, refrigerate the tree tomato juice for about 30 minutes to chill it. Alternatively, you can serve it immediately over ice cubes for a refreshing cold drink.

Serve Jugo de Tomate de Árbol:
10. Pour the tree tomato juice into glasses.
11. Optionally, garnish each glass with a sprig of fresh mint for added freshness.

Café de Loja (Loja Coffee)

Ingredients:
- Freshly roasted Loja coffee beans
- Fresh, cold water
- Coffee grinder

- Coffee maker (e.g., drip brew, French press, or espresso machine)
- Filter (if using drip brew)

Instructions:

Choose High-Quality Coffee Beans:
1. Start with freshly roasted Café de Loja coffee beans. The quality of the beans is essential for a rich and flavorful cup of coffee.

Measure Coffee Beans:
2. Measure the coffee beans according to your preferred coffee-to-water ratio. A common starting point is about 1 to 2 tablespoons of coffee grounds for every 6 ounces (180 ml) of water. Adjust the amount to suit your taste.

Grind the Coffee Beans:
3. Grind the coffee beans just before brewing. The grind size should match your chosen brewing method:
- Coarse grind for French press
- Medium grind for drip brew
- Fine grind for espresso

Boil Water:
4. Use fresh, cold water and bring it to a boil. Let the water cool for a moment after boiling to achieve the ideal brewing temperature of around 195°F to 205°F (90°C to 96°C).

Prepare Your Coffee Maker:
5. Depending on your chosen brewing method, set up your coffee maker:
- **Drip Brew**: Place a filter in the drip brew basket and add the ground coffee.
- **French Press**: Add the coffee grounds to the French press.
- **Espresso Machine**: Fill the portafilter with coffee grounds and tamp them down evenly.

Brew the Coffee:
6. Pour the hot water over the coffee grounds in a steady, circular motion, ensuring that all the grounds are saturated. Use the appropriate water-to-coffee ratio for your method.
7. Allow the coffee to steep or brew for the recommended time:
- French Press: About 4 minutes
- Drip Brew: Follow the manufacturer's instructions.
- Espresso: Brew until you've extracted the desired amount of coffee (usually around 25-30 seconds).

Serve and Enjoy Café de Loja:

8. Once the coffee is brewed, pour it into your favorite coffee mug.
9. Enjoy Café de Loja black or with your preferred additions, such as milk, cream, sugar, or sweeteners.

Note: For the most authentic experience, consider enjoying Café de Loja without cream or sugar to fully appreciate its unique flavor profile.

SAUCES AND CONDIMENTS

Ají (Ecuadorian Hot Sauce)

Ingredients:
- 4-6 hot chili peppers (aji peppers or similar, adjust to your desired spice level)
- 2 cloves garlic, minced
- 1 small red onion, finely chopped
- 2 tomatoes, finely chopped
- 1/4 cup fresh cilantro leaves, chopped
- 2 tablespoons white vinegar
- 2 tablespoons water
- Salt to taste

Instructions:

Prepare the Chili Peppers:
1. Begin by wearing gloves, especially if you're working with very spicy chili peppers, to protect your hands from the heat.
2. Wash the chili peppers thoroughly under cold running water.
3. Remove the stems and seeds from the chili peppers if you prefer a milder heat. Leaving some seeds will make the sauce spicier.

Blend the Ingredients:
4. In a blender or food processor, combine the chili peppers, minced garlic, and a pinch of salt. Pulse until you have a coarse paste. Be cautious when opening the blender, as the spicy fumes can be strong.

Mix with Additional Ingredients:
5. Transfer the chili pepper paste to a mixing bowl.
6. Add the finely chopped red onion, tomatoes, and cilantro to the bowl.
7. Stir in the white vinegar and water.
8. Season the mixture with salt to taste, adding more if needed.

Adjust Spice Level and Consistency:
9. Taste the ají sauce and adjust the spice level by adding more chili pepper seeds or paste if desired.
10. If you prefer a thinner consistency, you can add a bit more water or vinegar.

Serve Ají:
11. Allow the ají sauce to sit for at least 15-30 minutes before serving. This allows the flavors to meld and mellow.
12. Serve ají as a versatile condiment alongside Ecuadorian dishes. It adds a spicy kick and vibrant flavor to soups, stews, grilled meats, and more.

Storage: Store any leftover ají sauce in an airtight container in the refrigerator. It can be kept for several days and often becomes even more flavorful with time.

Chimichurri

Ingredients:
- 1 cup fresh parsley leaves, finely chopped
- 4 cloves garlic, minced
- 1/4 cup red wine vinegar
- 1/2 cup extra-virgin olive oil
- 1 teaspoon dried oregano
- 1 teaspoon red pepper flakes (adjust to taste)
- Salt and black pepper to taste
- 1 small red onion, finely chopped (optional)
- 1 bell pepper, finely chopped (optional)

Instructions:
Prepare the Chimichurri:
1. In a mixing bowl, combine the finely chopped parsley and minced garlic.
2. Add the red wine vinegar and dried oregano to the bowl, stirring to combine.
3. Gradually drizzle in the extra-virgin olive oil while whisking

vigorously to emulsify the dressing.
4. Season the chimichurri with red pepper flakes, salt, and black pepper to taste. Adjust the amount of red pepper flakes to your preferred level of spiciness.

Optional Ingredients:
5. For a variation, you can add finely chopped red onion and bell pepper to the chimichurri for added flavor and texture. Stir these optional ingredients into the sauce.

Let the Flavors Marry:
6. Allow the chimichurri to sit at room temperature for at least 30 minutes to an hour before serving. This resting period allows the flavors to meld and develop.

Serve Chimichurri:
7. Serve chimichurri as a flavorful condiment for grilled meats, such as steak, chicken, or lamb. It's also excellent with grilled vegetables, roasted potatoes, or as a dipping sauce for bread.
8. Store any leftover chimichurri in an airtight container in the refrigerator. It can be kept for several days and is great for adding a burst of flavor to various dishes.

Salsa de Maní (Peanut Sauce)

Ingredients:
- 1 cup unsalted roasted peanuts
- 2 cloves garlic, minced
- 1 small onion, finely chopped
- 1 tablespoon vegetable oil
- 1/2 cup water
- 1/2 cup milk
- Salt and pepper to taste
- 1 teaspoon achiote or annatto powder (optional, for color)
- 1/2 teaspoon ground cumin (optional, for extra flavor)
- 1/4 teaspoon cayenne pepper or red pepper flakes (adjust to taste, for heat)

Instructions:
Prepare the Peanut Sauce:
1. In a blender or food processor, add the roasted peanuts and pulse until they are finely ground into a peanut meal. Set aside.
2. In a saucepan over medium heat, heat the vegetable oil.
3. Add the minced garlic and finely chopped onion to the saucepan.

Sauté until the onion becomes translucent and fragrant.
4. Add the ground peanuts to the saucepan and stir well to combine with the garlic and onion. Cook for about 2-3 minutes, allowing the peanuts to release their oils and flavors.
5. Gradually add the water and milk to the peanut mixture, stirring continuously to create a smooth sauce.
6. If using, add the achiote or annatto powder, ground cumin, and cayenne pepper (or red pepper flakes) to the sauce. Stir well to incorporate the spices and enhance the flavor and color of the sauce.
7. Reduce the heat to low and let the sauce simmer for about 10-15 minutes, stirring occasionally. This will allow the flavors to meld, and the sauce will thicken to your desired consistency.
8. Taste the peanut sauce and season with salt and pepper according to your preference. Adjust the level of spiciness by adding more cayenne pepper or red pepper flakes if desired.

Serve Salsa de Maní:
9. Salsa de Maní can be served warm or at room temperature. It pairs exceptionally well with grilled meats, poultry, or as a dipping sauce for fried foods like empanadas, yuca, or plantains.
10. Store any leftover peanut sauce in an airtight container in the refrigerator. It can be reheated gently before serving.

Salsa de Cilantro (Cilantro Sauce)

Ingredients:
- 1 cup fresh cilantro leaves and stems, roughly chopped
- 2 cloves garlic, minced
- 1/2 cup mayonnaise
- 2 tablespoons plain yogurt or sour cream
- 1 tablespoon lime juice
- 1/2 teaspoon ground cumin
- Salt and pepper to taste
- 1/4 teaspoon cayenne pepper (optional, for a hint of heat)
- Water (as needed to adjust consistency)

Instructions:

Prepare the Cilantro Sauce:
1. In a blender or food processor, combine the roughly chopped cilantro, minced garlic, mayonnaise, plain yogurt or sour cream, lime juice, and ground cumin.

2. Blend the ingredients until you have a smooth and vibrant green sauce. If the sauce is too thick, you can add a small amount of water to achieve your desired consistency.
3. Season the cilantro sauce with salt and pepper to taste. Adjust the spiciness by adding cayenne pepper if desired.

Taste and Adjust:
4. Taste the cilantro sauce and make any necessary adjustments. You can add more lime juice for acidity, more salt and pepper for seasoning, or additional cayenne pepper for extra heat.

Serve Cilantro Sauce:
5. Cilantro sauce is best served chilled. Refrigerate it for at least 30 minutes before serving to allow the flavors to meld.
6. Use this versatile sauce as a refreshing condiment for a wide range of dishes, including grilled meats, seafood, tacos, roasted vegetables, and as a dipping sauce for empanadas or plantains.
7. Store any leftover cilantro sauce in an airtight container in the refrigerator. It can be kept for several days and used to add a burst of fresh flavor to various meals.

BREAD AND SNACKS

Pan de Yuca (Cheese Bread)

Ingredients:
- 2 cups yuca flour (cassava flour)
- 1 1/2 cups grated queso fresco (fresh cheese)
- 1/2 cup grated mozzarella cheese (optional, for added cheesiness)
- 2 large eggs
- 1/4 cup butter, melted
- 1/4 cup whole milk
- 1/2 teaspoon salt
- 1/4 teaspoon baking powder
- 1/4 teaspoon sugar (optional, for a hint of sweetness)

Instructions:
Prepare the Dough:
1. In a mixing bowl, combine the yuca flour, grated queso fresco, and grated mozzarella cheese (if using). Mix these dry ingredients together.
2. In a separate bowl, whisk the eggs until they are well beaten.
3. Add the melted butter, whole milk, salt, baking powder, and sugar (if using) to the beaten eggs. Stir to combine the wet ingredients.
4. Pour the wet mixture into the bowl with the dry ingredients.
5. Use your hands or a spatula to knead and mix the dough thoroughly until it comes together. The dough should be smooth

and slightly sticky.

Shape the Cheese Bread:
6. Preheat your oven to 375°F (190°C) and line a baking sheet with parchment paper.
7. Take small portions of the dough and roll them into small balls, about 1 to 1.5 inches in diameter. You can oil your hands lightly to prevent sticking.
8. Place the dough balls on the prepared baking sheet, leaving some space between them.

Bake Pan de Yuca:
9. Bake the cheese bread in the preheated oven for about 15-20 minutes or until they turn golden brown and have a slightly crispy exterior.
10. Once done, remove the pan de yuca from the oven and let them cool for a few minutes before serving.

Serve Pan de Yuca:
11. Pan de Yuca is best enjoyed warm. Serve them as a delightful snack, side dish, or appetizer. They're perfect on their own or with a cup of hot coffee or tea.

Note: Pan de Yuca is traditionally made with yuca flour, which is different from wheat flour, so it has a unique texture and flavor. If you can't find yuca flour, you can use tapioca flour as a substitute.

Pan de Pincho (Skewer Bread)

Ingredients:
For the Dough:
- 4 cups all-purpose flour
- 1 tablespoon active dry yeast
- 1 teaspoon sugar
- 1 teaspoon salt
- 2 tablespoons vegetable oil
- 1 1/2 cups warm water (approximately)

For the Skewers:
- Wooden skewers, soaked in water for 30 minutes to prevent burning
- Additional vegetable oil for brushing

Instructions:

Prepare the Dough:
1. In a small bowl, combine the warm water, sugar, and active dry

yeast. Let it sit for about 5-10 minutes until the mixture becomes frothy, indicating that the yeast is active.
2. In a large mixing bowl, combine the flour and salt.
3. Gradually add the yeast mixture and vegetable oil to the dry ingredients, stirring as you go.
4. Knead the dough for about 5-7 minutes until it's smooth and elastic. You can add a little more flour or water if necessary to achieve the right consistency. The dough should be slightly sticky but manageable.
5. Form the dough into a ball and place it in a lightly oiled bowl. Cover it with a clean kitchen towel or plastic wrap and let it rise in a warm place for about 1-1.5 hours or until it has doubled in size.

Shape the Skewer Bread:
6. After the dough has risen, punch it down to release any air bubbles.
7. Pinch off portions of the dough and shape them into small cylinders or balls, about the size of a golf ball.
8. Thread the dough pieces onto the soaked wooden skewers, leaving some space in between each piece to allow for expansion during cooking.

Cook the Skewer Bread:
9. Preheat a grill or stovetop griddle to medium-high heat. Brush it lightly with vegetable oil to prevent sticking.
10. Carefully place the skewers on the grill or griddle and cook for about 5-7 minutes on each side, or until the bread is golden brown and has a slightly crispy exterior. Keep turning the skewers to ensure even cooking.

Serve Pan de Pincho:
11. Remove the skewer bread from the grill or griddle and let them cool for a few minutes before serving.
12. Serve Pan de Pincho as a delightful snack or side dish. These skewer breads are perfect for dipping in sauces, soups, or enjoying on their own.

Tortillas de Maíz (Corn Tortillas)

Ingredients:
- 2 cups masa harina (corn masa flour)
- 1 1/2 cups warm water (approximately)

- 1/2 teaspoon salt (optional)

Instructions:

Prepare the Dough:

1. In a mixing bowl, combine the masa harina and salt (if using).
2. Gradually add the warm water to the masa harina, stirring continuously with a wooden spoon or your hands.
3. Knead the dough for about 2-3 minutes until it's smooth and pliable. If the dough is too dry, add a bit more warm water; if it's too sticky, sprinkle in a little more masa harina.
4. Form the dough into a ball and cover it with a damp cloth or plastic wrap. Let it rest for about 15-20 minutes. This resting period allows the masa to absorb the water fully and makes the dough easier to work with.

Shape the Tortillas:

5. After the dough has rested, pinch off small portions and roll them into balls, about the size of a golf ball.
6. Place a ball of dough between two sheets of plastic wrap or parchment paper. Using a tortilla press or a flat-bottomed heavy object, such as a cast-iron skillet, press the dough ball to flatten it into a round tortilla. Aim for a thickness of about 1/8 to 1/4 inch.

Cook the Tortillas:

7. Heat a griddle or large skillet over medium-high heat.
8. Carefully peel one of the plastic wrap or parchment paper sheets from a flattened tortilla and place the tortilla on the hot, ungreased griddle or skillet.
9. Cook the tortilla for about 1-2 minutes on each side, or until it puffs up slightly and develops light brown spots.
10. Remove the cooked tortilla from the griddle and keep it warm by wrapping it in a clean kitchen towel or a tortilla warmer. Repeat the process with the remaining dough balls.

Serve Corn Tortillas:

11. Serve the warm corn tortillas as a versatile accompaniment to a wide range of Ecuadorian dishes. They are perfect for wrapping around grilled meats, beans, cheese, or using as a base for various toppings.

Note: Corn tortillas can be made with just masa harina and water, but the optional addition of salt can enhance the flavor. You can also experiment by adding a bit of oil or fat for a softer texture.

Arepas (Cornmeal Patties)

Ingredients:
- 2 cups pre-cooked white or yellow cornmeal (masarepa)
- 2 1/2 cups warm water
- 1 teaspoon salt
- 1 cup grated queso fresco (fresh cheese) or mozzarella cheese (optional)
- Vegetable oil for cooking

Instructions:

Prepare the Arepa Dough:
1. In a mixing bowl, combine the pre-cooked cornmeal (masarepa) and salt.
2. Gradually add the warm water to the cornmeal, stirring continuously with a wooden spoon or your hands.
3. Knead the dough for about 2-3 minutes until it's smooth and pliable. The dough should be moist but not sticky. If it's too dry, add a bit more warm water; if it's too sticky, sprinkle in a little more cornmeal.
4. Add the grated queso fresco or mozzarella cheese (if using) to the dough. Knead it in until it's evenly distributed.

Shape and Cook the Arepas:
5. Divide the dough into portions and roll them into balls, about the size of a golf ball.
6. Flatten each dough ball into a round patty, about 1/2 to 3/4 inch thick. You can shape them with your hands or use a tortilla press if available.

Cook the Arepas:
7. Heat a griddle or large skillet over medium-high heat and lightly grease it with vegetable oil.
8. Carefully place the arepas on the hot griddle or skillet and cook for about 4-5 minutes on each side, or until they develop a golden-brown crust and sound hollow when tapped.
9. If needed, you can adjust the heat to ensure they cook evenly without burning.

Serve Arepas:
10. Remove the cooked arepas from the griddle and let them cool slightly.
11. Slice open each arepa horizontally, creating a pocket, and fill it

with your favorite ingredients. Common fillings include cheese, avocado, beans, shredded meat, or eggs.
12. Serve the arepas warm, and enjoy these delicious, versatile cornmeal patties as a satisfying meal or snack.

Note: Arepas can be filled with a wide variety of ingredients, making them a versatile and customizable dish. Feel free to get creative with your fillings!

PRESERVES

Mermelada de Guayaba (Guava Jam)

Ingredients:
- 4 cups ripe guavas, peeled, seeds removed, and chopped
- 2 cups granulated sugar
- 1/4 cup water
- 2 tablespoons freshly squeezed lemon juice

Instructions:

Prepare the Guavas:
1. Begin by washing the guavas thoroughly under cold running water.
2. Peel the guavas and cut them in half. Remove the seeds using a spoon or your fingers, and chop the flesh into small pieces. You should have about 4 cups of chopped guava.

Cook the Guava Jam:
3. In a large, heavy-bottomed saucepan, combine the chopped guavas, granulated sugar, and water.
4. Place the saucepan over medium-high heat and stir to dissolve the sugar.
5. Once the mixture comes to a boil, reduce the heat to low and let it simmer gently for about 30-45 minutes, or until the guava mixture thickens and reaches a jam-like consistency. Stir occasionally during this process.
6. As the guava jam cooks, it will become thicker and turn a deep,

rich color.
7. About 5 minutes before the jam is done, add the freshly squeezed lemon juice and stir it in. This will brighten the flavor and help set the jam.

Test for Doneness:
8. To test if the jam is ready, place a small amount on a chilled plate. Allow it to cool for a moment, and then push your finger through it. If it wrinkles and holds its shape, it's ready. If not, continue simmering for a few more minutes and test again.

Jar and Store the Guava Jam:
9. While the jam is still hot, carefully transfer it to sterilized jars. Leave about 1/4 inch of headspace at the top.
10. Seal the jars tightly with lids while they are still hot to create a vacuum seal. You can use the water bath canning method for long-term storage or store the sealed jars in the refrigerator for shorter-term use.

Enjoy Guava Jam:
11. Once the jam has cooled and set, it's ready to enjoy! Spread it on toast, biscuits, or use it as a sweet filling for pastries. Guava jam is a delightful addition to your breakfast or snack time.

Note: Make sure to follow proper canning procedures if you plan to store the guava jam at room temperature for an extended period. This will help ensure its long-term shelf stability.

Mermelada de Tomate de Árbol (Tree Tomato Jam)

Ingredients:
- 2 cups ripe tree tomatoes (tamarillos), peeled and chopped
- 1 1/2 cups granulated sugar
- 1/4 cup water
- 2 tablespoons freshly squeezed lemon juice

Instructions:
Prepare the Tree Tomatoes:
1. Begin by washing the tree tomatoes under cold running water.
2. To peel them, cut a shallow "X" on the bottom of each tree tomato. Submerge them in a pot of boiling water for about 1-2 minutes or until you notice the skin starting to loosen.
3. Quickly transfer the tree tomatoes to a bowl of ice water to cool.

Once they're cool enough to handle, you can easily peel off the skin starting from the "X" you cut.
4. Chop the peeled tree tomatoes into small pieces. You should have about 2 cups of chopped tree tomato flesh.

Cook the Tree Tomato Jam:
5. In a large, heavy-bottomed saucepan, combine the chopped tree tomatoes, granulated sugar, and water.
6. Place the saucepan over medium-high heat and stir to dissolve the sugar.
7. Once the mixture comes to a boil, reduce the heat to low and let it simmer gently for about 30-45 minutes, or until the tree tomato mixture thickens and reaches a jam-like consistency. Stir occasionally during this process.
8. As the tree tomato jam cooks, it will become thicker and develop a rich color.
9. About 5 minutes before the jam is done, add the freshly squeezed lemon juice and stir it in. This will enhance the flavor and help set the jam.

Test for Doneness:
10. To test if the jam is ready, place a small amount on a chilled plate. Allow it to cool for a moment, and then push your finger through it. If it wrinkles and holds its shape, it's ready. If not, continue simmering for a few more minutes and test again.

Jar and Store the Tree Tomato Jam:
11. While the jam is still hot, carefully transfer it to sterilized jars. Leave about 1/4 inch of headspace at the top.
12. Seal the jars tightly with lids while they are still hot to create a vacuum seal. You can use the water bath canning method for long-term storage or store the sealed jars in the refrigerator for shorter-term use.

Enjoy Tree Tomato Jam:
13. Once the jam has cooled and set, it's ready to enjoy! Spread it on toast, use it as a glaze for meats, or pair it with cheese.

HOLIDAY SPECIALTIES

Rosca de Pascua (Easter Bread)

Ingredients:
For the Dough:
- 4 cups all-purpose flour
- 1/2 cup granulated sugar
- 1/2 cup unsalted butter, softened
- 4 large eggs
- 1/2 cup warm milk
- 2 teaspoons active dry yeast
- 1/2 teaspoon salt
- 1 teaspoon vanilla extract
- Zest of 1 lemon or orange (optional)

For the Decoration:
- 1 beaten egg (for egg wash)
- Colorful sprinkles or candied fruit (for decoration)
- Hard-boiled colored eggs (optional, for placing on the bread)

Instructions:

Prepare the Dough:
1. In a small bowl, dissolve the active dry yeast in the warm milk. Let it sit for about 5-10 minutes until it becomes frothy, indicating that the yeast is active.
2. In a large mixing bowl, combine the flour, sugar, and salt. Create a well in the center.

3. Add the softened butter, eggs, yeast mixture, vanilla extract, and lemon or orange zest (if using) into the well.
4. Begin mixing the ingredients together until a dough forms.
5. Knead the dough on a lightly floured surface for about 10-15 minutes until it becomes smooth and elastic. You can also use a stand mixer with a dough hook attachment.
6. Form the dough into a ball and place it in a lightly oiled bowl. Cover it with a clean kitchen towel or plastic wrap and let it rise in a warm place for about 1-2 hours, or until it has doubled in size.

Shape the Rosca:
7. After the dough has risen, punch it down to release any air bubbles.
8. Divide the dough into two portions. Roll each portion into a long rope, about 24 inches in length.
9. Twist the two ropes together to form a braided ring or circle. Pinch the ends together to seal them.

Decorate the Rosca:
10. Preheat your oven to 350°F (175°C).
11. Brush the beaten egg over the entire surface of the Rosca. This will give it a glossy finish when baked.
12. Decorate the Rosca with colorful sprinkles or candied fruit.
13. If you'd like to include hard-boiled colored eggs, place them in the spaces between the dough twists on the Rosca.

Bake the Rosca:
14. Place the decorated Rosca on a baking sheet lined with parchment paper.
15. Bake in the preheated oven for about 25-30 minutes, or until the Rosca is golden brown and sounds hollow when tapped on the bottom.

Serve Rosca de Pascua:
16. Allow the Rosca to cool on a wire rack before serving.
17. Rosca de Pascua is traditionally enjoyed during Easter celebrations. Share this delicious Easter bread with family and friends as a symbol of togetherness and renewal.
18. Don't forget to retrieve and enjoy the hard-boiled eggs from the Rosca.

Note: Some variations of Rosca de Pascua include a hidden figurine and a dried bean inside the bread. The person who finds the figurine is said to have good luck, and the one who finds the bean is responsible for providing the Rosca the following year.

Colada Morada (Day of the Dead Beverage)

Ingredients:
- 2 cups purple corn flour (harina de maíz morado)
- 8 cups water
- 1 cup panela or brown sugar (piloncillo), grated or chopped
- 4 cinnamon sticks
- 4 cloves
- 4 allspice berries (pimienta dulce)
- 4 guava leaves (hojas de guayaba)
- 4 naranjilla leaves (hojas de naranjilla) or substitute with orange leaves
- 1 cup fresh pineapple, chopped
- 1/2 cup strawberries, chopped
- 1/2 cup blueberries
- 1/2 cup blackberries
- 1/2 cup raspberries
- Juice of 4 limes
- Juice of 2 oranges
- Juice of 2 lemons
- 1/2 cup diced pineapple or pineapple chunks (for garnish)

Instructions:

Prepare the Purple Corn Base:
1. In a large pot, combine the purple corn flour and water. Stir well to dissolve the flour.
2. Add the panela or brown sugar to the pot and mix until it's fully incorporated into the liquid.
3. Add the cinnamon sticks, cloves, and allspice berries to the pot, as well as the guava leaves and naranjilla leaves.
4. Place the pot over medium heat and bring the mixture to a boil. Once it's boiling, reduce the heat to low and let it simmer for about 30 minutes. Stir occasionally to prevent sticking.
5. After 30 minutes, remove the pot from the heat. Allow the mixture to cool to room temperature, and then strain it through a fine-mesh sieve or cheesecloth into a large bowl. Discard the solid ingredients.

Prepare the Fruits and Citrus Juices:

6. In a separate bowl, combine the chopped fresh pineapple, strawberries, blueberries, blackberries, and raspberries.
7. In another bowl, squeeze the juice from the limes, oranges, and lemons.

Combine and Chill:
8. Pour the strained purple corn base into a large pitcher or punch bowl.
9. Add the mixed fruit and the citrus juices to the pitcher. Stir well to combine.
10. Taste the Colada Morada and adjust the sweetness and acidity to your preference by adding more panela or citrus juice if needed.
11. Chill the Colada Morada in the refrigerator for at least 2 hours before serving. It's even better if you let it chill overnight.

Serve Colada Morada:
12. When serving, add diced pineapple or pineapple chunks to each glass or cup.
13. Colada Morada is traditionally enjoyed during the Day of the Dead (Día de los Difuntos) celebrations in Ecuador. It's a delicious and comforting beverage that pays tribute to loved ones who have passed away.
14. Share this flavorful and vibrant drink with family and friends as you remember and celebrate the lives of those who came before us.

Note: Colada Morada is often served with guaguas de pan (sweet bread shaped like dolls or babies) during the Day of the Dead festivities in Ecuador.

Guaguas de Pan (Bread Babies for All Souls' Day)

Ingredients:

For the Dough:
- 4 cups all-purpose flour
- 1/2 cup granulated sugar
- 1/2 cup unsalted butter, softened
- 1/2 cup warm milk
- 4 large eggs
- 2 teaspoons active dry yeast
- 1/2 teaspoon salt

- 1 teaspoon vanilla extract
- Zest of 1 lemon or orange (optional)

For the Filling:
- 1/2 cup guava paste or fig jam (for filling)

For Decoration:
- Colored sprinkles (optional)
- Egg wash (1 beaten egg)

Instructions:

Prepare the Dough:

1. In a small bowl, dissolve the active dry yeast in the warm milk. Let it sit for about 5-10 minutes until it becomes frothy, indicating that the yeast is active.
2. In a large mixing bowl, combine the flour, sugar, and salt. Create a well in the center.
3. Add the softened butter, eggs, yeast mixture, vanilla extract, and lemon or orange zest (if using) into the well.
4. Begin mixing the ingredients together until a dough forms.
5. Knead the dough on a lightly floured surface for about 10-15 minutes until it becomes smooth and elastic. You can also use a stand mixer with a dough hook attachment.
6. Form the dough into a ball and place it in a lightly oiled bowl. Cover it with a clean kitchen towel or plastic wrap and let it rise in a warm place for about 1-2 hours, or until it has doubled in size.

Shape Guaguas de Pan:

7. After the dough has risen, punch it down to release any air bubbles.
8. Divide the dough into small portions, about the size of a golf ball. The number of portions depends on the size of the guaguas you want to make.
9. Take each portion and flatten it into a round disk in the palm of your hand.
10. Place a small amount of guava paste or fig jam in the center of each disk.
11. Carefully fold the dough over the filling, shaping it into a baby figure. You can create simple baby shapes or get creative with your designs.

Decorate Guaguas de Pan:

12. Preheat your oven to 350°F (175°C).

13. Brush the guaguas with the egg wash, which will give them a glossy finish when baked.
14. Decorate the guaguas with colored sprinkles, if desired.

Bake Guaguas de Pan:

15. Place the decorated guaguas on a baking sheet lined with parchment paper.
16. Bake in the preheated oven for about 15-20 minutes, or until the guaguas are golden brown and sound hollow when tapped on the bottom.

Serve Guaguas de Pan:

17. Allow the guaguas to cool on a wire rack before serving.
18. Guaguas de Pan are traditionally enjoyed during All Souls' Day (Día de los Difuntos) celebrations in Ecuador. They are a sweet and symbolic treat that honors departed loved ones.
19. Share these delightful bread babies with family and friends as you pay tribute to the memories of those who have passed away.

Note: Guaguas de Pan can be made in various sizes and shapes, and their decorations can be as simple or intricate as you like. Use your creativity to craft unique and meaningful bread babies for your All Souls' Day celebration.

COCKTAILS

Pisco Sour

Ingredients:
- 2 oz (60 ml) Pisco
- 1 oz (30 ml) fresh lime juice
- 3/4 oz (22 ml) simple syrup (equal parts sugar and water)
- 1/2 oz (15 ml) pasteurized egg white (optional)
- Angostura bitters (for garnish)
- Ice

Instructions:
1. Chill a cocktail glass in the freezer for about 10 minutes before making the drink.
2. In a cocktail shaker, combine the Pisco, fresh lime juice, simple syrup, and pasteurized egg white if using. The egg white gives the cocktail a smooth and frothy texture but is optional.
3. Fill the shaker with ice, ensuring it's at least halfway full.
4. Secure the shaker's lid and shake vigorously for about 10-15 seconds. This helps to chill the cocktail and create a frothy texture.
5. Strain the cocktail into the chilled glass.
6. Garnish the Pisco Sour with a few drops of Angostura bitters on top. You can create decorative patterns or simply let the bitters float on the foam.
7. Serve immediately and enjoy your classic Pisco Sour!

Pisco is a type of brandy that is popular in both Peru and Ecuador. There are slight variations in the preparation of Pisco Sour between the two countries, but this recipe reflects the Ecuadorian style. Feel free to adjust the sweetness or sourness to your taste by adding more or less simple syrup or lime juice.

Caipirinha

Ingredients:
- 2 oz (60 ml) Cachaça (Brazilian sugarcane spirit)
- 1 lime, cut into small wedges
- 2 teaspoons granulated sugar
- Ice cubes
- Lime slices or wedges for garnish (optional)

Instructions:
1. Begin by washing the lime thoroughly and cutting it into small wedges. Remove any seeds if necessary.
2. Place the lime wedges and granulated sugar in a rocks glass (also known as an Old Fashioned glass).
3. Use a muddler to gently muddle (crush) the lime wedges and sugar together. This releases the lime's juice and combines it with the sugar. Be careful not to over-muddle, as you don't want to release too much bitterness from the lime peel.
4. Fill the glass with ice cubes.
5. Pour the Cachaça over the ice and lime mixture.
6. Use a cocktail stirrer or a long spoon to gently stir the ingredients together, ensuring that the lime and sugar are well incorporated with the Cachaça.
7. Garnish the Caipirinha with a lime slice or wedge if desired.
8. Serve immediately, and enjoy this refreshing cocktail!

Note: The traditional Caipirinha is made with Cachaça, but you can also make variations using other spirits like vodka (Caipiroska) or rum (Caipirissima). Adjust the sweetness to your liking by adding more or less sugar. Some variations also include additional fruits or flavors, like passion fruit or strawberries, for a twist on the classic recipe.

Margarita de Maracuyá (Passion Fruit Margarita)

Ingredients:
- 2 oz (60 ml) silver tequila
- 1 oz (30 ml) triple sec or orange liqueur
- 1 oz (30 ml) freshly squeezed lime juice
- 1 oz (30 ml) freshly squeezed passion fruit juice (maracuyá)
- 1/2 oz (15 ml) simple syrup (equal parts sugar and water)
- Ice
- Salt or Tajín (chili-lime seasoning) for rimming the glass (optional)
- Lime wheel or wedge for garnish (optional)

Instructions:
1. If desired, rim a chilled margarita glass with salt or Tajín. To do this, rub the rim of the glass with a lime wedge, then dip it into a shallow plate of salt or Tajín.
2. In a cocktail shaker, combine the silver tequila, triple sec, freshly squeezed lime juice, passion fruit juice, and simple syrup.
3. Fill the shaker with ice, ensuring it's at least halfway full.
4. Secure the shaker's lid and shake vigorously for about 10-15 seconds. This helps to chill the cocktail and combine the ingredients.
5. Strain the margarita into the prepared glass filled with ice.
6. If desired, garnish the Passion Fruit Margarita with a lime wheel or wedge.
7. Serve immediately and enjoy the tropical flavors of this delightful cocktail!

Note: Adjust the sweetness to your liking by adding more or less simple syrup. You can also experiment with different rimming options, such as using a mixture of salt and Tajín for a spicy kick.

CONVERSION TABLES

Volume Conversions:
- 1 teaspoon (tsp) = 5 milliliters (ml)
- 1 tablespoon (tbsp) = 15 milliliters (ml)
- 1 fluid ounce (fl oz) = 30 milliliters (ml)
- 1 cup (c) = 240 milliliters (ml)
- 1 pint (pt) = 480 milliliters (ml)
- 1 quart (qt) = 960 milliliters (ml)
- 1 gallon (gal) = 3,840 milliliters (ml)

Weight Conversions:
- 1 ounce (oz) = 28.35 grams (g)
- 1 pound (lb) = 453.59 grams (g)
- 1 gram (g) = 0.0353 ounces (oz)
- 1 kilogram (kg) = 1,000 grams (g)
- 1 kilogram (kg) = 2.2046 pounds (lb)

Temperature Conversions:
- Fahrenheit to Celsius: (°F - 32) × 5/9 = °C
- Celsius to Fahrenheit: (°C × 9/5) + 32 = °F

Common Oven Temperatures:
- 300°F = 150°C (low oven)
- 350°F = 180°C (moderate oven)
- 375°F = 190°C
- 400°F = 200°C (moderate-high oven)
- 450°F = 230°C (hot oven)

Liquid Measurements:

- 1 liter (L) = 1,000 milliliters (ml)
- 1 milliliter (ml) = 0.001 liters (L)

Dry Measurements:
- 1 milligram (mg) = 0.001 grams (g)
- 1 gram (g) = 0.001 kilograms (kg)

Common Ingredient Conversions:
- 1 stick of butter = 1/2 cup = 8 tablespoons = 4 ounces
- 1 cup of flour = 120 grams
- 1 cup of sugar = 200 grams
- 1 cup of rice = 200 grams
- 1 cup of water = 240 milliliters

Length Conversions:
- 1 inch (in) = 2.54 centimeters (cm)
- 1 foot (ft) = 30.48 centimeters (cm)
- 1 meter (m) = 100 centimeters (cm)
- 1 meter (m) = 3.281 feet (ft)

These conversion tables should help you convert measurements easily while cooking or baking in the kitchen. Keep in mind that some recipes may provide measurements in different units, so having these conversions at hand can be quite handy for precise cooking and baking.

Made in the USA
Columbia, SC
27 November 2024